Two Plays

SARA
MINNA VON BARNHELM

First published in 1990 by Absolute Classics, an imprint of
Absolute Press, 14 Widcombe Crescent, Bath, England

© Anthony Meech (Minna von Barnhelm)

Series Editor: Giles Croft

Cover and text design: Ian Middleton

Photoset and printed by WBC Print, Bristol
Bound by W.H. Ware & Sons, Clevedon

ISBN 0 948230 29 0

VAT Registration Number: 8/T/56479/A
A Pentos Company

HODGES *f*IGGIS

**57-58 Dawson Street
Dublin 2 Ireland
Telephone: 01 774754**

Registered in Ireland 56361
VAT Registration Number: 8/T/56479/A
A Pentos Company

HODGES *f*IGGIS

**57-58 Dawson Street
Dublin 2 Ireland
Telephone: 01 774754**

Registered in Ireland 56361
VAT Registration Number: 8/T/56479/A
A Pentos Company

```
       HODGES FIGGIS THE BOOKSTORE
            57/58 Dawson Street
                 Dublin 2
D027
BARGAINS                    £4.99
D027
BARGAINS                    £2.99
D027
BARGAINS                    £2.99
D027
BARGAINS                    £1.99
D027
BARGAINS                    £1.99
D027
BARGAINS                    £1.99
D027
BARGAINS                    £1.99
D027
BARGAINS                    £1.99
                  TOT:      £20.92
F8    H VOUC AMT:           £10.00
F1    CASH  AMT:            £11.00
REC: 109781:140195:1247:02TGHT
    PLEASE KEEP YOUR RECEIPT
        VAT No. 8/T/56479/A
```

SARA

Translated by Ernest Bell

MINNA VON BARNHELM

Translated by Anthony Meech

Two plays by
Gotthold Ephraim Lessing

a b s o l u t e   c l a s s i c

INTRODUCTION

The son of a Protestant pastor, Gotthold Ephraim Lessing was born in Kamenz, Saxony in 1729. It was intended that he should follow his father into the church, and he matriculated at Leipzig University to read theology. But he abandoned thought of a career in the church, preferring the study of medicine, while spending much of his time in and around the theatre. Backstage with the touring company of Caroline Neuber, he learned the basics of the craft of the stage, and it was the Neuber company which produced Lessing's first attempts at playwriting.

It was in 1755, however, that Lessing for the first time broke new ground in the theatre. Influenced by the novels of Richardson, (in particular CLARISSA), he introduced bourgeois tragedy on to the German stage in MISS SARA SAMPSON, the first tragedy in German to be taken from contemporary life and written in unstilted prose dialogue.

His intention of travelling in Europe was thwarted by the onset of the Seven Years War, during which Lessing spent time in both Leipzig and Berlin, writing both plays and literary criticism. For five years from 1760 he served as secretary to General Taudenzien in Breslau, seeing the conduct of the war at first hand.

In 1766 he published his treatise LAOKOON, which established him at the forefront of European art criticism. In this essay he opposes to Winkelmann's view of classical art as serene and still an interpretation of classical sculpture as a tense balance of powerful forces. This rediscovery of the energy in classical art was to prove an inspiration for the young writers of the *Sturm und Drang* movement in the next decade.

The next year he published MINNA VON BARNHELM, which has maintained for two centuries its place as one of the most popular comedies in the German theatre repertoire, being regularly revived, both in the Federal Republic and the GDR. Set against a background of the end of the Seven Years War, Lessing's play shows how a witty, and wily Saxony woman can ultimately trick her stiff-necked Prussian officer fiancé into admitting his true feelings of love for her.

His major contribution to theatre criticism THE HAMBURG

DRAMATURGY (1767-8) was the result of his acting as resident
critic to the then newly established National Theatre in Hamburg.
The Dramaturgy starts as a series of reviews of the ill-fated theatre's
productions, but Lessing soon digresses into discussions on the nature
and role of theatre and drama, especially tragedy, and suggestions for
the improvement of the German theatre repertoire. In his analysis of
catharsis, he rejects the view, current at the time, that tragedy
achieves its effect on the audience by way of pity and terror. For
terror, he, more correctly, substitutes fear. The audience is to feel pity
for the hero in his suffering; the fear is the pity of the audience
turned on itself. Lessing, the quintessential bourgeois, largely ignored
the admiration which other critics had seen as an essential reaction of
an audience towards a tragic hero. Instead he suggests that our pity is
more likely to be excited by the sufferings of our social equals, rather
than of a remote nobleman or a mythological figure. In this, and his
insistence that the aim of tragedy, as of all genres of poetry, should be
the moral improvement of the audience, he provides the theoretical
basis of the German domestic tragedy.

He rejects the contemporary French adherence to the Aristotelian
Unities, and suggests that the English drama would prove a better
model for the Germans in their attempts to establish a national theatre
repertoire. He goes so far as to declare that Shakespeare remains truer
to the Greeks in breaking the Unities than the French who attempt
strictly to observe them. Shakespeare stays true to the spirit of
Aristotle because his theatre is "characteristic" of its age and people,
as the classical Greek theatre described by Aristotle was of its age,
where the French neo-classical theatre is not.

In 1770 he took up a position as librarian to the Duke of Brunswick at
Wolfenbüttel, and in 1772 published his own domestic tragedy – a
version of the Virginia story – EMILIA GALOTTI, a play which had
a major influence on subsequent writers including both Goethe and
Schiller.

After an extended tour of Italy as mentor to the Duke's son, he
married at the age of forty-seven, but was devastated when, only two
years later, his wife died in childbirth. He withdrew into his work as a
librarian, whilst engaging in protracted theological disputes in which
he espoused the cause of tolerance against orthodoxy. The theatrical
result of these concerns, and his last play, was NATHAN THE
WISE, an allegorical verse drama centring on the Jew, Nathan, and
preaching tolerance of and respect for all religions. Not performed in

his lifetime, NATHAN THE WISE was first successfully staged by Goethe at Weimar in 1801, since when it has frequently been revived on the German stage – most significantly after the defeat of the Nazis in 1945.

At the end of THE HAMBURG DRAMATURGY, Lessing writes that he is "neither an actor nor a poet", and suggests that his plays be seen as exemplars to act as stimuli for subsequent, greater writers of true genius. This they certainly did, and still do. But Lessing's modest assessment of himself is unfair. He was a playwright of considerable gifts and the outstanding critic of his age.

He died, at Wolfenbüttel, at the age of 52.

ANTHONY MEECH

SARA

The British Première production of SARA was toured by the Cheek byJowl Theatre Company in the spring of 1990. It opened at the International Theatre Festival in Montevideo, Uruguay on 18th April 1990, with the following company:

SIR WILLIAM SAMPSON	Daniel Thorndike
WAITWELL	Peter Needham
LANDLORD	Max Burrows
MELLEFONT	Raad Rawi
NORTON	Duncan Duff
BETTY	Charlotte Medcalf
SARA SAMPSON	Rachel Joyce
MARWOOD	Sheila Gish
HANNAH	Pat O'Toole
ARABELLA	Isabel Hernandez
DIRECTOR	Declan Donnellan
DESIGNER	Nick Ormerod
MUSIC DIRECTOR	Paddy Cunneen
MOVEMENT DIRECTOR	Jane Gibson
LIGHTING DESIGNER	Rick Fisher
COMPANY STAGE MANAGER	Louise Yeomans
DEPUTY STAGE MANAGER	Martin Lloyd Evans
TOURING ELECTRICIAN	Judith Greenwood
WARDROBE MISTRESS	Christine Maddison
WARDROBE SUPERVISOR	Angie Burns

SARA is the fifth European masterpiece to be given its British Première by Cheek by Jowl. Others include ANDROMACHE by Racine (France 1667, Britain 1984), THE CID by Corneille (France 1636, Britain 1986), A FAMILY AFFAIR by Ostrovsky (Russia 1850, Britain 1988), published by Absolute Press, and THE DOCTOR OF HONOUR by Calderon de la Barca (Spain 1635, Britain 1989).

ACT ONE

SCENE ONE

A room in an inn.

Sir William Sampson, Waitwell.

SIR WILLIAM: My daughter, here? Here in this wretched inn?

WAITWELL: No doubt, Mellefont has purposely selected the most wretched one in the town. The wicked always seek the darkness, because they are wicked. But what would it help them, could they even hide themselves from the whole world? Conscience after all is more powerful than the accusations of a world. Ah, you are weeping again, again, Sir! – Sir!

SIR WILLIAM: Let me weep, my honest old servant! Or does she not, do you think, deserve my tears?

WAITWELL: Alas! She deserves them, were they tears of blood.

SIR WILLIAM: Well, let me weep!

WAITWELL: The best, the loveliest, the most innocent child that ever lived beneath the sun, must thus be led astray! Oh, my Sara, my little Sara! I have watched thee grow; a hundred times have I carried thee as a child in these arms, have I admired thy smiles, thy lispings. From every childish look beamed forth the dawn of an intelligence, a kindliness, a –

SIR WILLIAM: Oh, be silent! Does not the present rend my heart enough? Will you make my tortures more infernal still by recalling past happiness? Change your tone, if you will do me a service. Reproach me, make of my tenderness a crime, magnify my daughter's fault; fill me with abhorrence of her, if you can; stir up anew my revenge against her cursed seducer; say, that Sara never was virtuous, since she so lightly ceased to be so; say that she never loved me, since she clandestinely forsook me!

WAITWELL: If I said that, I should utter a lie, a shameless, wicked lie. It might come to me again on my deathbed, and I,

old wretch, would die in despair. No, little Sara has
loved her father; and doubtless, doubtless she loves him
yet. If you will only be convinced of this, I shall see
her again in your arms this very day.

SIR WILLIAM: Yes, Waitwell, of this alone I ask to be convinced. I
cannot any longer live without her; she is the support
of my age, and if she does not help to sweeten the sad
remaining days of my life, who shall do it? If she loves
me still, her error is forgotten. It was the error of a
tender-hearted maiden, and her flight was the result of
her remorse. Such errors are better than forced virtues.
Yet I feel, Waitwell, I feel it, even were there errors
real crimes, premeditated vices – even then I should
forgive her. I would rather be loved by a wicked
daughter, than by none at all.

WAITWELL: Dry your tears, dear sir! I hear someone. It will be the
landlord coming to welcome us.

SCENE TWO

The Landlord, Sir William Sampson, Waitwell.

LANDLORD: So early, gentlemen, so early? You are welcome;
welcome, Waitwell! You have doubtless been travelling
all night! Is that the gentleman of whom you spoke to
me yesterday?

WAITWELL: Yes, it is he, and I hope that in accordance with what
we settled –

LANDLORD: I am entirely at your service, my lord. What is it to me
whether I know or not what cause has brought you
hither, and why you wish to live in seclusion in my
house? A landlord takes his money and lets his guests do
as they think best. Waitwell, it is true, has told me that
you wish to observe the stranger a little, who has been
staying here for a few weeks with his young wife, but I
hope that you will not cause him any annoyance. You
would bring my house into ill repute and certain people
would fear to stop here. Men like us must live on
people of all kinds.

SIR WILLIAM: Do not fear; only conduct me to the room which

Waitwell has ordered for me; I come here for an
honourable purpose.

LANDLORD: I have no wish to know your secrets, my lord!
Curiosity is by no means a fault of mine. I might for
instance have known long ago, who the stranger is, on
whom you want to keep a watch, but I have no wish to
know. This much however I have discovered, that he
must have eloped with the young lady. The poor little
wife – or whatever she may be! – remains the whole day
long locked up in her room, and cries.

SIR WILLIAM: And cries?

LANDLORD: Yes, and cries; but, my lord, why do your tears fall?
The young lady must interest you deeply. Surely you
are not –

WAITWELL: Do not detain him any longer!

LANDLORD: Come, come! One wall only will separate you from the
lady in whom you are so much interested, and who
may be –

WAITWELL: You mean then at any cost to know, who –

LANDLORD: No, Waitwell! I have no wish to know anything.

WAITWELL: Make haste, then, and take us to our rooms, before the
whole house begins to stir.

LANDLORD: Will you please follow me, then, my lord?

Exeunt.

SCENE THREE

Mellefont's room.

Mellefont, Norton.

MELLEFONT: *(In dressing-room, sitting in an easy chair.)* Another
night, which I could not have spent more cruelly on
the rack! – *(Calls)* Norton! – I must make haste to get
sight of a face or two. If I remained alone with my
thoughts any longer, they might carry me too far. Hey,

Norton! He is still asleep. But is not it cruel of me, not to let the poor devil sleep? How happy he is! However, I do not wish anyone about me to be happy! Norton!

NORTON: *(Coming)* Sir!

MELLEFONT: Dress me! – Oh, no sour looks please! When I shall be able to sleep longer myself I will let you do the same. If you wish to do your duty, at least have pity on me.

NORTON: Pity, sir! Pity on you? I know better where pity is due.

MELLEFONT: And where then?

NORTON: Ah, let me dress you and don't ask.

MELLEFONT: Confound it! Are *your* reproofs then to awaken together with my conscience? I understand you; I know on whom you expend your pity. But I will do justice to her and to myself. Quite right, do not have any pity on me! Curse me in your heart; but – curse yourself also!

NORTON: Myself also?

MELLEFONT: Yes, because you serve a miserable wretch, whom earth ought not to bear, and because you have made yourself a partaker in his crimes.

NORTON: I made myself a partaker in your crimes? In what way?

MELLEFONT: By keeping silent about them.

NORTON: Well, that is good! A word would have cost me my neck in the heat of your passions. And, besides, did I not find you already so bad, when I made your acquaintance, that all hope of amendment was vain? What a life I have seen you leading from the first moment! In the lowest society of gamblers and vagrants – I call them what they were without regard to their knightly titles and such like – in this society you squandered a fortune which might have made a way for you to an honourable position. And your culpable intercourse with all sorts of women, especially with the wicked Marwood –

MELLEFONT: Restore me – restore me to that life. It was virtue compared with the present one. I spent my fortune; well! The punishment follows, and I shall soon enough feel all the severity and humiliation of want. I

associated with vicious women; that may be. I was
myself seduced more often than I seduced others; and
those whom I did seduce wished it. But – I still had no
ruined virtue upon my conscience. I had carried off no
Sara from the house of a beloved father and forced her
to follow a scoundrel, who was no longer free. I had
. . . who comes so early to me?

SCENE FOUR

Betty, Mellefont, Norton.

NORTON: It is Betty.

MELLEFONT: Up already, Betty? How is your mistress?

BETTY: How is she? *(Sobbing)* It was long after midnight before
             I could persuade her to go to bed. She slept a few
             moments; but God, what a sleep that must have been!
             She started suddenly, sprang up and fell into my arms,
             like one pursued by a murderer. She trembled, and a
             cold perspiration started on her pale face. I did all I
             could to calm her, but up to this morning she has only
             answered me with silent tears. At length she sent me
             several times to your door to listen whether you were
             up. She wishes to speak to you. You alone can
             comfort her. O do so, dearest sir, do so! My heart will
             break, if she continues to fret like this.

MELLEFONT: Go, Betty! Tell her, I shall be with her in a moment.

BETTY: No, she wishes to come to you herself.

MELLEFONT: Well, tell her, then, that I am awaiting her –

             Exit Betty.

SCENE FIVE

Mellefont, Norton.

NORTON: O God, the poor young lady!

MELLEFONT: Whose feelings is this exclamation of yours meant to

rouse? See, the first tear which I have shed since my
childhood is running down my cheek. A bad
preparation for receiving one who seeks comfort. But
why does she seek it from me? Yet where else shall she
seek it? I must collect myself *(Drying his eyes.)* Where
is the old firmness with which I could see a beautiful
eye in tears? Where is the gift of dissimulation gone by
which I could be and could say whatsoever I wished?
She will come now and weep tears that brook no
resistance. Confused and ashamed I shall stand before
her; like a convicted criminal I shall stand before her.
Counsel me, what shall I do? What shall I say?

NORTON: You shall do what she asks of you!

MELLEFONT: I shall then perpetrate a fresh act of cruelty against her.
She is wrong to blame me for delaying a ceremony
which cannot be performed in this country without the
greatest injury to us.

NORTON: Well, leave it, then. Why do we delay? Why do you let
one day after the other pass, and one week after the
other? Just give me the order, and you will be safe on
board tomorrow! Perhaps her grief will not follow her
over the ocean; she may leave part of it behind, and in
another land may –

MELLEFONT: I hope that myself. Silence! She is coming! How my
heart throbs!

SCENE SIX

Sara, Mellefont, Norton.

MELLEFONT: *(Advancing towards her.)* You have had a restless night,
dearest Sara.

SARA: Alas, Mellefont, if it were nothing but a restless night.

MELLEFONT: *(To his servant.)* Leave us!

NORTON: *(Aside, in going.)* I would not stay if I was paid in gold
for every moment.

SCENE SEVEN

Sara, Mellefont.

MELLEFONT: You are faint, dearest Sara! You must sit down!

SARA: *(Sits down.)* I trouble you very early! Will you forgive
             me that with the morning I again begin my complaints?

MELLEFONT: Dearest Sara, you mean to say that you cannot forgive
             me, because another morning has dawned, and I have
             not yet put an end to your complaints?

SARA: What is there that I would not forgive you? You know
             what I have already forgiven you. But the ninth week,
             Mellefont! The ninth week begins today, and this
             miserable house still sees me in just the same position as
             on the first day.

MELLEFONT: You doubt my love?

SARA: I doubt your love? No, I feel my misery too much, too
             much to wish to deprive myself of this last and only
             solace.

MELLEFONT: How, then, can you be uneasy about the delay of a
             ceremony?

SARA: Ah, Mellefont! Why is it that we think so differently
             about this ceremony! Yield a little to the woman's way
             of thinking! I imagine in it a more direct consent from
             Heaven. In vain did I try again, only yesterday, in the
             long tedious evening, to adopt your ideas, and to banish
             from my breast the doubt which just now – not for the
             first time, you have deemed the result of my distrust. I
             struggled with myself; I was clever enough to deafen
             my understanding; but my heart and my feeling quickly
             overthrew this toilsome structure of reason.
             Reproachful voices roused me from my sleep, and my
             imagination united with them to torment me. What
             pictures, what dreadful pictures hovered about me! I
             would willingly believe them to be dreams –

MELLEFONT: What? Could my sensible Sara believe them to be
             anything else? Dreams, my dearest, dreams! – How
             unhappy is man! – Did not his Creator find tortures
             enough for him in the realm of reality? Had he also to

create in him the still more spacious realm of
imagination in order to increase them?

SARA: Do not accuse Heaven! It has left the imagination
in our power. She is guided by our acts; and when
these are in accordance with our duties and with virtue
the imagination serves only to increase our peace and
happiness. A single act, Mellefont, a single blessing
bestowed upon us by a messenger of peace, in the name
of the Eternal One, can restore my shattered
imagination again. Do you still hesitate to do a few days
sooner for love of me, what in any case you mean to do
at some future time? Have pity on me, and consider
that, although by this you may be freeing me only from
torments of the imagination, yet these imagined
torments are torments, and are real torments for her
who feels them. Ah! could I but tell you the terrors of
the last night half as vividly as I have felt them.
Wearied with crying and grieving – my only
occupations – I sank down on my bed with half-closed
eyes. My nature wished to recover itself a moment, to
collect new tears. But hardly asleep yet, I suddenly saw
myself on the steepest peak of a terrible rock. You went
on before, and I followed with tottering, anxious steps,
strengthened now and then by a glance which you
threw back upon me. Suddenly I heard behind me a
gentle call, which bade me stop. It was my father's
voice – I unhappy one, can I forget nothing which is
his? Alas if his memory renders him equally cruel
service; if he too cannot forget me! – But he has
forgotten me. Comfort! Cruel comfort for his Sara! –
But, listen, Mellefont! In turning round to this well-
known voice, my foot slipped; I reeled, and was on the
point of falling down the precipice, when just in time, I
felt myself held back by one who resembled myself. I
was just returning her my passionate thanks, when she
drew a dagger from her bosom. "I saved you," she cried,
"to ruin you!" She lifted her armed hand – and –! I
awoke with the blow. Awake, I still felt all the pain
which a mortal stab must give, without the pleasure
which it brings – the hope for the end of grief in the
end of life.

MELLEFONT: Ah! dearest Sara, I promise you the end of your grief, without the end of your life, which would certainly be the end of mine also. Forget the terrible tissue of a meaningless dream!

SARA: I look to you for the strength to be able to forget it. Be it love or seduction, happiness or unhappiness which threw me into your arms, I am yours in my heart and will remain so for ever. But I am not yet yours in the eyes of that Judge, who has threatened to punish the smallest transgressions of His law –

MELLEFONT: Then may all the punishment fall upon me alone!

SARA: What can fall upon you, without touching me too? But do not misinterpret my urgent request! Another woman, after having forfeited her honour by an error like mine, might perhaps only seek to regain a part of it by a legal union. I do not think of that, Mellefont, because I do not wish to know of any other honour in this world than that of loving you. I do not wish to be united to you for the world's sake but for my own. And I will willingly bear the shame of not appearing to be so, when I am united to you. You need not then, if you do not wish, acknowledge me to be your wife, you may call me what you will! I will not bear your name; you shall keep our union as secret as you think good, and may I always be unworthy of it, if I ever harbour the thought of drawing any other advantage from it than the appeasing of my conscience.

MELLEFONT: Stop, Sara, or I shall die before your eyes. How wretched I am, that I have not the courage to make you more wretched still! Consider that you have given yourself up to my guidance; consider that it is my duty to look to our future, and that I must at present be deaf to your complaints, if I will not hear you utter more grievous complaints throughout the rest of your life. Have you then forgotten what I have so often represented to you in justification of my conduct?

SARA: I have not forgotten it, Mellefont! You wish first to secure a certain bequest. You wish first to secure temporal goods, and you let me forfeit eternal ones, perhaps, through it.

MELLEFONT: Ah, Sara! If you were as certain of all temporal goods as your virtue is of the eternal ones –

SARA: My virtue? Do not say that word! Once it sounded sweet to me, but now a terrible thunder rolls in it!

MELLEFONT: What? Must he who is to be virtuous, never have committed a trespass? Has a single error such fatal effect that it can annihilate a whole course of blameless years? If so, no one is virtuous; virtue is then a chimera, which disperses in the air, when one thinks that one grasps it most firmly; if so, there is no Wise Being who suits our duties to our strength; if so, there is. . . . I am frightened at the terrible conclusions in which your despondency must involve you. No, Sara, you are still the virtuous Sara that you were before your unfortunate acquaintance with me. If you look upon yourself with such cruel eyes, with what eyes must you regard me!

SARA: With the eyes of love, Mellefont!

MELLEFONT: I implore you, then, on my knees I implore you for the sake of this love, this generous love which overlooks all my unworthiness, to calm yourself! Have patience for a few days longer!

SARA: A few days! How long even a single day is!

MELLEFONT: Cursed bequest! Cursed nonsense of a dying cousin, who would only leave me his fortune on the condition that I should give my hand to a relation who hates me as much as I hate her! To you, inhuman tyrants of our freedom, be imputed all the misfortune, all the sin, into which your compulsion forces us! Could I but dispense with this degrading inheritance! As long as my father's fortune sufficed for my maintenance, I always scorned it, and did not even think it worthy of mentioning. But now, now, when I should like to possess all the treasures of the world only to lay them at the feet of my Sara, now, when I must contrive at least to let her appear in the world as befits her station, now I must have recourse to it.

SARA: Which probably will not be successful after all.

MELLEFONT: You always forbode the worst. No, the lady whom this also concerns is not disinclined to enter into a sort of agreement with me. The fortune is to be divided, and as she cannot enjoy the whole with me, she is willing to let me buy my liberty with half of it. I am every hour expecting the final intelligence, the delay of which alone has so prolonged our sojourn here. As long as I receive it, we shall not remain here one moment longer. We will immediately cross to France, dearest Sara, where you shall find new friends, who already look forward to the pleasure of seeing and loving you. And these new friends shall be the witnesses of our union –

SARA: They shall be the witnesses of our union? Cruel man, our union, then, is not to be in my native land? I shall leave my country as a criminal? And as such, you think, I should have the courage to trust myself to the ocean. The heart of him must be calmer or more impious than mine, who, only for a moment, can see with indifference between himself and destruction, nothing but a quivering plank. Death would roar at me in every wave that struck against the vessel, every wind would howl its curses after me from my native shore, and the slightest storm would seem a sentence of death pronounced upon me. No, Mellefont, you cannot be so cruel to me! If I live to see the completion of this agreement, you must not grudge another day, to be spent here. This must be the day, on which you shall teach me to forget the tortures of all these tearful days. This must be the sacred day – alas! Which day will it be?

MELLEFONT: But do you consider, Sara, that our marriage here would lack those ceremonies which are due to it?

SARA: A sacred act does not acquire more force through ceremonies.

MELLEFONT: But –

SARA: I am astonished. You surely will not insist on such a trivial pretext? O Mellefont, Mellefont! Had I not made for myself an inviolable law, never to doubt the sincerity of your love, this circumstance might. . . But too much of this already, it might seem as if I had been doubting it even now.

MELLEFONT: The first moment of your doubt would be the last
moment of my life! Alas, Sara, what have I done,
that you should remind me even of the possibility of it?
It is true the confessions, which I have made to you
without fear, of my early excesses cannot do me
honour, but they should at least awaken confidence. A
coquettish Marwood held me in her meshes, because I
felt for her that which is so often taken for love which
it so rarely is. I should still bear her shameful fetters,
had not Heaven, which perhaps did not think my heart
quite unworthy to burn with better flames, taken pity
on me. To see you, dearest Sara, was to forget all
Marwoods! But how dearly have you paid for taking
me out of such hands! I had grown too familiar with
vice, and you know it too little –

SARA: Let us think no more of it.

SCENE EIGHT

Norton, Mellefont, Sara.

MELLEFONT: What do you want?

NORTON: While I was standing before the house, a servant gave
me this letter. It is directed to you, sir!

MELLEFONT: To me? Who knows my name here? *(Looking at the
letter.)* Good heavens!

SARA: You are startled.

MELLEFONT: But without cause, Sara, as I now perceive. I was
mistaken in the handwriting.

SARA: May the contents be as agreeable to you as you can
wish.

MELLEFONT: I suspect that they will be of very little importance.

SARA: One is less constrained when one is alone, so allow me
to retire to my room again.

MELLEFONT: You entertain suspicions, then, about it?

SARA: Not at all, Mellefont.

MELLEFONT: *(Going with her to the back of the stage.)* I shall be with
you in a moment, dearest Sara.

SCENE NINE

Mellefont, Norton.

MELLEFONT: *(Still looking at the letter.)* Just heaven!

NORTON: Woe to you, if it is only just!

MELLEFONT: Is it possible? I see this cursed handwriting again and
am not chilled with terror? Is it she? Is it not she?
Why do I still doubt? It is she! Alas, friend, a letter
from Marwood! What fury, what demon has betrayed
my abode to her? What does she still want from me?
Go, make preparations immediately that we may get
away from here. Yet stop! Perhaps it is unnecessary;
perhaps the contempt of my farewell letters has only
caused Marwood to reply with equal contempt. There,
open the letter; read it! I am afraid to do it myself.

NORTON: *(Reads)* "If you will deign, Mellefont, to glance at the
name which you will find at the bottom of the page, it
will be to me as though I had written you the longest
of letters."

MELLEFONT: Curse the name! Would I had never heard it! Would it
could be erased from the book of the living!

NORTON: *(Reads on.)* "The labour of finding you out has been
sweetened by the love which helped me in my search."

MELLEFONT: Love? Wanton creature! You profane the words which
belong to virtue alone.

NORTON: *(Continues)* "Love has done more still" –

MELLEFONT: I tremble –

NORTON: "It has brought me to you" –

MELLEFONT: Traitor, what are you reading? *(Snatches the letter from
his hand and reads himself.)* "I am here; and it rests with
you, whether you will await a visit from me, or whether
you will anticipate mine by one from you. Marwood."

What a thunderbolt! She is here! Where is she? She
shall atone for this audacity with her life!

NORTON: With her life? One glance from her and you will be
again at her feet. Take care what you do! You must not
speak with her, or the misfortunes of your poor young
lady will be complete.

MELLEFONT: O, wretched man that I am! No, I must speak with
her! She would go even into Sara's room in search of
me, and would vent all her rage on the innocent girl.

NORTON: But, sir –

MELLEFONT: Not a word! Let me see *(Looking at the letter.)* whether
she has given the address. Here it is! Come, show me
the way!

     Exeunt.

END OF ACT ONE

ACT TWO

SCENE ONE

Marwood's room in another inn.

Marwood, (in negligée), Hannah.

MARWOOD: I hope Belfort has delivered the letter at the right address, Hannah?

HANNAH: He has.

MARWOOD: To him himself?

HANNAH: To his servant.

MARWOOD: I am all impatience to see what effect it will have. Do I not seem a little uneasy to you, Hannah? And I am so. The traitor! But gently! I must not on any account give way to anger. Forbearance, love, entreaty are the only weapons which I can use against him, if I rightly understand his weak side.

HANNAH: But if he should harden himself against them?

MARWOOD: If he should harden himself against them? Then I shall not be angry. I shall rave! I feel it, Hannah, and I would rather do so to begin with.

HANNAH: Calm yourself! He may come at any moment.

MARWOOD: I only hope he may come; I only hope he has not decided to await me on his own ground. But do you know, Hannah, on what I chiefly found my hopes of drawing away the faithless man from this new object of his love? On our Bella!

HANNAH: It is true, she is a little idol to him; and there could not have been a happier idea than that of bringing her with you.

MARWOOD: Even if his heart should be deaf to an old love, the language of blood will at least be audible to him. He tore the child from my arms a short time ago under the pretext of wishing to give her an education such as she

could not have with me. It is only by an artifice that I
have been able to get her again from the lady who had
charge of her. He had paid more than a year in
advance, and had given strict orders the very day
before his flight that they should by no means give
admission to a certain Marwood, who would perhaps
come and give herself out as mother of the child. From
this order I see the distinction which he draws between
us. He regards Arabella as a precious portion of
himself, and me as an unfortunate creature, of whose
charms he has grown weary.

HANNAH: What ingratitude!

MARWOOD: Ah, Hannah! Nothing more infallibly draws down
ingratitude, than favours for which no gratitude would
be too great. Why have I shown him these fatal
favours? Ought I not to have foreseen that they could
not always retain their value with him; that their value
rested on the difficulty in the way of their enjoyment,
and that the latter must disappear with the charm of
our looks which the hand of time imperceptibly but
surely effaces?

HANNAH: You, Madam, have not anything to fear for a long time
from this dangerous hand! To my mind your beauty is
so far from having passed the point of its brightest
bloom, that it is rather advancing towards it, and would
enchain fresh hearts for you every day if you only
would give it the permission.

MARWOOD: Be silent, Hannah! You flatter me on an occasion which
makes me suspicious of any flattery. It is nonsense to
speak of new conquests, if one has not even sufficient
power to retain possession of those which one has
already made.

SCENE TWO

A servant, Marwood, Hannah.

SERVANT: Someone wishes to have the honour of speaking with
you.

MARWOOD: Who is it?

SERVANT:	I suppose it is the gentleman to whom the letter was addressed. At least the servant to whom I delivered it is with him.
MARWOOD:	Mellefont! – Quick, bring him up! *(Exit Servant.)* Ah, Hannah! He is here now! How shall I receive him? What shall I say? What look shall I put on? Is this calm enough? Just see!
HANNAH:	Anything but calm.
MARWOOD:	This, then?
HANNAH:	Throw a little sweetness into it.
MARWOOD:	So, perhaps?
HANNAH:	Too sad.
MARWOOD:	Would this smile do?
HANNAH:	Perfectly – only less constrained – he is coming.

SCENE THREE

Mellefont, Marwood, Hannah.

MELLEFONT:	*(Entering with wild gestures).* Ha! Marwood –
MARWOOD:	*(Running to meet him smiling, and with open arms.)* Ah, Mellefont!
MELLEFONT:	*(Aside)* The murderess! What a look!
MARWOOD:	I must embrace you, faithless, dear fugitive! Share my joy with me! Why do you tear yourself from my caresses?
MELLEFONT:	I expected, Marwood, that you would receive me differently.
MARWOOD:	Why differently? With more love, perhaps? With more delight? Alas, how unhappy I am, that I cannot express all that I feel! Do you not see, Mellefont, do you not see that joy, too, has its tears? Here they fall, the offspring of sweetest delight! But alas, vain tears! His hand does not dry you!
MELLEFONT:	Marwood, the time is gone, when such words would

have charmed me. You must speak now with me in
another tone. I come to hear your last reproaches and
to answer them.

MARWOOD: Reproaches? What reproaches should I have for you,
Mellefont? None!

MELLEFONT: Then you might have spared yourself the journey, I
should think.

MARWOOD: Dearest, capricious heart. Why will you forcibly compel
me to recall a trifle which I forgave you the same
moment I heard of it? Does a passing infidelity which
your gallantry, but not your heart, has caused, deserve
these reproaches? Come, let us laugh at it!

MELLEFONT: You are mistaken; my heart is more concerned in it,
than it ever was in all our love affairs, upon which I
cannot now look back but with disgust.

MARWOOD: Your heart, Mellefont, is a good little fool. It lets your
imagination persuade it to whatever it will. Believe me,
I know it better than you do yourself! Were it not the
best, the most faithful of hearts, should I take such
pains to keep it?

MELLEFONT: To keep it? You have never possessed it, I tell you.

MARWOOD: And I tell you, that in reality I possess it still!

MELLEFONT: Marwood! If I knew that you still possessed one single
fibre of it, I would tear it out of my breast here before
your eyes.

MARWOOD: You would see that you were tearing mine out at the
same time. And then, then these hearts would at last
attain that union which they have sought so often upon
our lips.

MELLEFONT: *(Aside)* What a serpent! Flight will be the best thing
here. – Just tell me briefly, Marwood, why you have
followed me, and what you still desire of me! But tell it
me without this smile, without this look, in which a
whole hell of seduction lurks and terrifies me.

MARWOOD: *(Insinuatingly)* Just listen, my dear Mellefont! I see
your position now. Your desires and your taste are at
present your tyrants. Never mind, one must let them

wear themselves out. It is folly to resist them. They are
most safely lulled to sleep, and at last even conquered,
by giving them free scope. They wear themselves away.
Can you accuse me, my fickle friend, of ever having
been jealous, when more powerful charms than mine
estranged you from me for a time? I never grudged
you the change, by which I always won more than
I lost. You returned with new ardour, with new
passion to my arms, in which with light bonds, and
never with heavy fetters I encompassed you. Have I
not often even been your confidante though you had
nothing to confide but the favours which you stole
from me, in order to lavish them on others. Why
should you believe then, that I would now begin to
display a capriciousness just when I am ceasing, or,
perhaps have already ceased, to be justified in it. If
your ardour for the pretty country girl has not yet
cooled down, if you are still in the first fever of your
love for her; if you cannot yet do without the
enjoyment she gives you; who hinders you from
devoting yourself to her, as long as you think good?
But must you on that account make such rash projects,
and purpose to fly from the country with her?

MELLEFONT: Marwood! You speak in perfect keeping with your
character, the wickedness of which I never understood
so well as I do now, since, in the society of a virtuous
woman, I have learned to distinguish love from
licentiousness.

MARWOOD: Indeed! Your new mistress is then a girl of fine moral
sentiments, I suppose? You men surely cannot know
yourselves what you want. At one time you are pleased
with the most wanton talk and the most unchaste jests
from us, at another time we charm you when we talk
nothing but virtue, and seem to have all the seven sages
on our lips. But the worst is, that you get tired of one
as much as the other. We may be foolish or reasonable,
worldly or spiritual; our efforts to make you constant
are lost either way. The turn will come to your
beautiful saint soon enough. Shall I give you a little
sketch? Just at present you are in the most passionate
paroxysm over her. I allow this two or at the most
three days more. To this will succeed a tolerably calm

love; for this I allow a week. The next week you will
only think occasionally of this love. In the third week,
you will have to be reminded of it; and when you have
got tired of being thus reminded, you will so quickly
see yourself reduced to the most utter indifference, that
I can hardly allow the fourth week for this final change.
This would be about a month altogether. And this
month, Mellefont, I will overlook with the greatest of
pleasure; but you will allow that I must not lose sight
of you.

MELLEFONT: You try all the weapons in vain which you remember to
have used successfully with me in bygone days. A
virtuous resolution secures me against both your
tenderness and your wit. However, I will not expose
myself longer to either. I go, and have nothing more to
tell you but that in a few days you shall know that I am
bound in such a manner as will utterly destroy all your
hope of my ever returning into your sinful slavery. You
will have learned my justification sufficiently from the
letter which I sent to you before my departure.

MARWOOD: It is well that you mention this letter. Tell me, who did
you get to write it?

MELLEFONT: Did not I write it myself?

MARWOOD: Impossible! The beginning of it, in which you reckoned
up – I do not know what sums – which you say you
have wasted with me, must have been written by an
innkeeper, and the theological part at the end by a
Quaker. I will now give you a serious reply to it. As to
the principal point, you well know that all the presents
which you have made are still in existence. I have never
considered your cheques or your jewels as my property,
and I have brought them all with me to return them
into the hands which entrusted them to me.

MELLEFONT: Keep them all, Marwood!

MARWOOD: I will not keep any of them. What right have I to them
without you yourself? Although you do not love me any
more, you must at least do me justice and not take me
for one of those venal females, to whom it is a matter
of indifference by whose booty they enrich themselves.
Come, Mellefont, you shall this moment be as rich

again as you perhaps might still be if you had not
known me; and perhaps, too, might *not* be.

MELLEFONT: What demon intent upon my destruction speaks
through you now! Voluptuous Marwood does not think
so nobly.

MARWOOD: Do you call that noble? I call it only just. No, Sir, no,
I do not ask that you shall account the return of your
gifts as anything remarkable. It costs me nothing, and I
should even consider the slightest expression of thanks
on your part as an insult, which could have no other
meaning than this: "Marwood, I thought you a base
deceiver; I am thankful that you have not wished to be
so towards me at least."

MELLEFONT: Enough, Madam, enough! I fly, since my unlucky
destiny threatens to involve me in a contest of
generosity, in which I should be most unwilling to
succumb.

MARWOOD: Fly, then! But take everything with you that could
remind me of you. Poor, despised, without honour, and
without friends, I will then venture again to awaken
your pity. I will show you in the unfortunate Marwood
only a miserable woman, who has sacrificed to you her
person, her honour, her virtue, and her conscience. I
will remind you of the first day, when you saw and
loved me; of the first, stammering, bashful confession
of your love, which you made me at my feet; of the
first assurance of my return of your love, which you
forced from me; of the tender looks, of the passionate
embraces, which followed, of the eloquent silence,
when each with busy mind divined the other's most
secret feelings, and read the most hidden thoughts of
the soul in the languishing eye; of the trembling
expectation of approaching gratification; of the
intoxication of its joys; of the sweet relaxation after the
fulness of enjoyment, in which the exhausted spirits
regained strength for fresh delights. I shall remind you
of all this, and then embrace your knees, and entreat
without ceasing for the only gift, which you cannot
deny me, and which I can accept without blushing –
for death from your hand.

MELLEFONT: Cruel one! I would still give even my life for you. Ask it, ask it, only do not any longer claim my love. I must leave you, Marwood, or make myself an object of loathing to the whole world. I am culpable already in that I only stand here and listen to you. Farewell, farewell!

MARWOOD: *(Holding him back.)* You must leave me? And what, then, do you wish, shall become of me? As I am now I am your creature; do, then, what becomes a creator; he may not withdraw his hand from the work until he wishes to destroy it utterly. Alas, Hannah, I see now, my entreaties alone are too feeble. Go, bring my intercessor, who will now, perhaps, return to me more than she ever received from me.

       Exit Hannah.

MELLEFONT: What intercessor, Marwood?

MARWOOD: Ah, an intercessor of whom you would only too willingly have deprived me. Nature will take a shorter road to your heart with her grievances.

MELLEFONT: You alarm me. Surely you have not –

SCENE FOUR

Arabella, Hannah, Mellefont, Marwood.

MELLEFONT: What do I see? It is she! Marwood, how could you dare to –

MARWOOD: Am I not her mother? Come, my Bella, see, here is your protector again, your friend, your. . . . Ah! his heart may tell him what more he can be to you than a protector and a friend.

MELLEFONT: *(Turning away his face.)* God, what shall I have to suffer here?

ARABELLA: *(Advancing timidly towards him.)* Ah, Sir! Is it you? Are you our Mellefont? No, Madam, surely, surely it is not he! Would he not look at me, if it were? Would he not hold me in his arms? He used to do so. What an

             unhappy child I am! How have I grieved him, this
             dear, dear man, who let me call him my father?

MARWOOD: You are silent, Mellefont? You grudge the innocent
             child a single look?

MELLEFONT: Ah!

ARABELLA: Why, he sighs, Madam! What is the matter with him?
             Cannot we help him? Cannot I? Nor you? Then let us
             sigh with him! Ah, now he looks at me! No, he looks
             away again! He looks up to Heaven! What does he
             want? What does he ask from Heaven? Would that
             Heaven would grant him everything, even if it refused
             me everything for it!

MARWOOD: Go, my child, go, fall at his feet! He wants to leave us,
             to leave us for ever.

ARABELLA: *(Falling on her knees before him.)* Here I am already.
             You will leave us? You will leave us for ever? Have not
             we already been without you for a little "for ever."
             Shall we have to lose you again? You have said so often
             that you loved us. Does one leave the people whom one
             loves? I cannot love you then, I suppose, for I should
             wish never to leave you. Never, and I never will leave
             you either.

MARWOOD: I will help you in your entreaties, my child! And you
             must help me too! Now, Mellefont, you see me too at
             your feet. . . .

MELLEFONT: *(Stopping her, as she throws herself at his feet.)*
             Marwood, dangerous Marwood! And you, too, my
             dearest Bella *(Raising her up.)*, you too are the enemy of
             your Mellefont?

ARABELLA: I your enemy?

MARWOOD: What is your resolve?

MELLEFONT: What it ought not to be, Marwood; what it ought not
             to be.

MARWOOD: *(Embracing him.)* Ah, I know that the honesty of your
             heart has always overcome the obstinacy of your
             desires.

MELLEFONT: Do not importune me any longer! I am already what you wish to make me; a perjurer, a seducer, a robber, a murderer!

MARWOOD: You will be so in imagination for a few days, and after that you will see that I have prevented you from becoming so in reality. You will return with us, won't you?

ARABELLA: *(Insinuatingly)* Oh yes, do!

MELLEFONT: Return with you! How can I?

MARWOOD: Nothing is easier, if you only wish it.

MELLEFONT: And my Sara –

MARWOOD: And your Sara may look to herself.

MELLEFONT: Ha! cruel Marwood, these words reveal the very bottom of your heart to me. And yet I, wretch, do not repent?

MARWOOD: If you had seen the bottom of my heart, you would have discovered that it has more true pity for your Sara than you yourself have. I say true pity; for your pity is egotistic and weak. You have carried this love-affair much too far. We might let it pass, that you as a man, who by long intercourse with our sex has become master in the art of seducing, used your superiority in dissimulation and experience against such a young maiden, and did not rest until you had gained your end. You can plead the impetuosity of your passion as your excuse. But, Mellefont, you cannot justify yourself for having robbed an old father of his only child, for having rendered to an honourable old man his few remaining steps to the grave harder and more bitter, for having broken the strongest ties of nature for the sake of your desires. Repair your error, then, as far as it is possible to repair it. Give the old man his support again, and send a credulous daughter back to her home, which you need not render desolate also, because you have dishonoured it.

MELLEFONT: This only was still wanting – that you should call in my conscience against me also. But even supposing what you say were just, must I not be brazenfaced if I should propose it myself to the unhappy girl?

MARWOOD :   Well, I will confess to you, that I have anticipated this
             difficulty, and considered how to spare you it. As soon
             as I learned your address, I informed her old father
             privately of it. He was beside himself with joy, and
             wanted to start directly. I wonder he has not yet
             arrived.

MELLEFONT : What do you say?

MARWOOD :   Just await his arrival quietly, and do not let the girl
             notice anything. I myself will not detain you any
             longer. Go to her again; she might grow suspicious. But
             I trust that I shall see you again to-day.

MELLEFONT : Oh, Marwood! With what feelings did I come to you,
             and with what must I leave you! A kiss, my dear Bella.

ARABELLA :   That was for you, now one for me! But come back
             again soon, do!

             Exit Mellefont.

SCENE FIVE

Marwood, Arabella, Hannah.

MARWOOD :   *(Drawing a deep breath.)* Victory, Hannah! But a hard
             victory! Give me a chair, I feel quite exhausted. *(Sitting
             down.)* He surrendered only just in time, if he had
             hesitated another moment, I should have shown him
             quite a different Marwood.

HANNAH :   Ah, Madam, what a woman you are! I should like to
             see the man who could resist you.

MARWOOD :   He has resisted me already too long. And assuredly,
             assuredly, I will not forgive him that he almost let me
             go down on my knees to him.

ARABELLA :   No, no! You must forgive him everything. He is so
             good, so good –

MARWOOD :   Be silent, little silly!

HANNAH :   I do not know on what side you did not attack him!
             But nothing, I think, touched him more, than the

disinterestedness with which you offered to return all
his presents to him.

MARWOOD: I believe so too. Ha! ha! ha! *(Contemptuously)*

HANNAH: Why do you laugh, Madam? You really risked a great
deal, if you were not in earnest about it. Suppose he
had taken you at your word?

MARWOOD: Oh, nonsense, one knows with whom one has to deal.

HANNAH: I quite admit that! But you too, my pretty Bella, did
your part excellently, excellently!

ARABELLA: How so? Could I do it, then, any other way? I had not
seen him for such a long time. I hope you are not
angry, Madam, that I love him so? I love you as much
as him, just as much.

MARWOOD: Very well, I will pardon you this time that you do not
love me better than him.

ARABELLA: *(Sobbing)* This time?

MARWOOD: Why, you are crying actually? What is it about?

ARABELLA: Ah, no! I am not crying. Do not get angry! I will love
you both so much, so much, that it will be impossible
to love either of you more.

MARWOOD: Very well.

ARABELLA: I am so unhappy.

MARWOOD: Now be quiet – but what is that?

SCENE SIX

Mellefont, Marwood, Arabella, Hannah.

MARWOOD: *(Rising)* Why do you come back again so soon,
Mellefont?

MELLEFONT: *(Passionately)* Because I needed but a few moments to
recover my senses.

MARWOOD: Well?

MELLEFONT: I was stunned, Marwood, but not moved! You have had all your trouble in vain. Another atmosphere than this infectious one of your room has given me back my courage and my strength, to withdraw my foot in time from this dangerous snare. Were the tricks of a Marwood not sufficiently familiar to me, unworthy wretch that I am?

MARWOOD: *(Impatiently)* What language is that?

MELLEFONT: The language of truth and anger.

MARWOOD: Gently, Mellefont! Or I too shall speak in the same language.

MELLEFONT: I return only in order not to leave you one moment longer under a delusion with regard to me, which must make me despicable even in your eyes.

ARABELLA: *(Timidly)* Oh, Hannah!

MELLEFONT: Look at me as madly as you like. The more madly the better! Was it possible that I could hesitate only for one moment between a Marwood and a Sara, and that I had well nigh decided for the former?

ARABELLA: Oh, Mellefont!

MELLEFONT: Do not tremble, Bella! For your sake too I came back. Give me your hand, and follow me without fear!

MARWOOD: *(Stopping them.)* Whom shall she follow, traitor?

MELLEFONT: Her father!

MARWOOD: Her father!

MARWOOD: Go, pitiable wretch, and learn first to know her mother.

MELLEFONT: I know her. She is a disgrace to her sex.

MARWOOD: Take her away, Hannah!

MELLEFONT: *(Attempting to stop her.)* Remain here, Bella.

MARWOOD: No force, Mellefont, or –

Exeunt Hannah and Arabella.

SCENE SEVEN

MARWOOD: Now we are alone! Say now once more, whether you are determined to sacrifice me for a foolish girl?

MELLEFONT: *(Bitterly)* Sacrifice you? You recall to my mind that impure animals were also sacrificed to the ancient gods.

MARWOOD: *(Mockingly)* Express yourself without these learned allusions.

MELLEFONT: I tell you, then, that I am firmly resolved never to think of you again but with the most fearful of curses. Who are you? And who is Sara? You are a voluptuous, egoistic, shameful strumpet, who certainly can scarcely remember any longer that she ever was innocent. I have nothing to reproach myself with but that I have enjoyed with you that which otherwise you would perhaps have let the whole world enjoy. You have sought me, not I you, and if I now know who Marwood is, I have paid for this knowledge dearly enough. It has cost me my fortune, my honour, my happiness –

MARWOOD: And I would that it might also cost you your eternal happiness. Monster! Is the devil worse than you, when he lures feeble mortals into crimes and himself accuses them afterwards for these crimes which are his own work! What is my innocence to you? What does it matter to you when and how I lost it. If I could not sacrifice my virtue, I have at least staked my good name for you. The former is no more valuable than the latter. What do I say? More valuable? Without it the former is a silly fancy, which brings one neither happiness nor guilt. The good name alone gives it some value, and can exist quite well without it. What did it matter what I was before I knew you, you wretch! It is enough that in the eyes of the world I was a woman without reproach. Through you only it has learned that I am not so; solely through my readiness to accept your heart, as I then thought, without your hand.

MELLEFONT: This very readiness condemns you, vile woman!

MARWOOD: But do you remember to what base tricks you owed

it? Was I not persuaded by you, that you could not be publicly united to me without forfeiting an inheritance which you wished to share with me only? Is it time now to renounce it? And to renounce it, not for me but for another!

MELLEFONT: It is a real delight to me to be able to tell you that this difficulty will soon be removed. Content yourself therefore with having deprived me of my father's inheritance, and let me enjoy a far smaller one with a more worthy wife.

MARWOOD: Ha! Now I see what it is that makes you so perverse. Well, I will lose no more words. Be it so! Be assured I shall do everything to forget you. And the first thing that I will do to this end, shall be this. You will understand me! Tremble for your Bella! Her life shall not carry the memory of my despised love down to posterity; my cruelty shall do it. Behold in me a new Medea!

MELLEFONT: *(Frightened)* Marwood! –

MARWOOD: Or, if you know a more cruel mother still, behold her cruelty doubled in me! Poison and dagger shall avenge me. But no, poison and dagger are tools too merciful for me! They would kill your child and mine too soon. I will not see it dead. I will see it dying! I will see each feature of the face which she has from you disfigured, distorted, and obliterated by slow torture. With eager hand will I part limb from limb, vein from vein, nerve from nerve, and will not cease to cut and burn the very smallest of them, even when there is nothing remaining but a senseless carcass! I – I shall at least feel in it – how sweet is revenge!

MELLEFONT: You are raving, Marwood –

MARWOOD: You remind me that my ravings are not directed against the right person. The father must go first! He must already be in yonder world, when, through a thousand woes the spirit of his daughter follows him. *(She advances towards him with a dagger which she draws from her bosom.)* So die, traitor!

MELLEFONT: *(Seizing her arm, and snatching the dagger from her).*

Insane woman! What hinders me now from turning the steel against you? But live, and your punishment shall be left for a hand void of honour.

MARWOOD: *(Wringing her hands.)* Heaven, what have I done? Mellefont –

MELLEFONT: Your grief shall not deceive me. I know well why you are sorry – not that you wished to stab me, but that you failed to do so.

MARWOOD: Give me back the erring steel! Give it me back, and you shall see for whom it was sharpened! For this breast alone, which for long has been too narrow for a heart which will rather renounce life than your love.

MELLEFONT: Hannah!

MARWOOD: What are you doing, Mellefont?

SCENE EIGHT

Hannah (in terror), Marwood, Mellefont.

MELLEFONT: Did you hear, Hannah, how madly your mistress was behaving? Remember that I shall hold you responsible for Arabella!

HANNAH: Madam, how agitated you are!

MELLEFONT: I will place the innocent child in safety immediately. Justice will doubtless be able to bind the murderous hands of her cruel mother. *(Going.)*

MARWOOD: Whither, Mellefont? Is it astonishing that the violence of my grief deprived me of my reason? Who forces me to such unnatural excess? Is it not you yourself? Where can Bella be safer than with me? My lips may rave, but my heart still remains the heart of a mother. Oh, Mellefont, forget my madness, and to excuse it think only of its cause.

MELLEFONT: There is only one thing which can induce me to forget it.

MARWOOD: And that is?

MELLEFONT: That you return immediately to London! I will send

Arabella there under another escort. You must by no means have anything further to do with her.

MARWOOD: Very well! I submit to everything; but grant me one single request more. Let me see your Sara once.

MELLEFONT: And what for?

MARWOOD: To read in her eyes my future fate. I will judge for myself whether she is worthy of such a breach of faith as you commit against me; and whether I may cherish the hope of receiving again, some day at any rate, a portion of your love.

MELLEFONT: Vain hope!

MARWOOD: Who is so cruel as to grudge even hope to the unhappy? I will not show myself to her as Marwood, but as a relation of yours. Announce me to her as such; you shall be present when I call upon her, and I promise you, by all that is sacred, to say nothing that is in any way displeasing to her. Do not refuse my request, for otherwise I might perhaps do all that is in my power to show myself to her in my true character.

MELLEFONT: Marwood! This request – *(After a moment's reflection.)* might be granted. – But will you then be sure to quit this spot?

MARWOOD: Certainly; yes, I promise you. Even more, I will spare you the visit from her father, if that is still possible.

MELLEFONT: There is no need of that! I hope that he will include me too in the pardon which he grants to his daughter. But if he will not pardon her, I too shall know how to deal with him. I will go and announce you to my Sara. Only keep your promise, Marwood.

Exit.

MARWOOD: Alas, Hannah, that our powers are not as great as our courage. Come, help me to dress. I do not despair of my scheme. If I could only make sure of him first. Come!

END OF ACT TWO

ACT THREE

SCENE ONE

A room in the first inn.

Sir William Sampson, Waitwell.

SIR WILLIAM: There, Waitwell, take this letter to her! It is the letter of an affectionate father, who complains of nothing but her absence. Tell her that I have sent you on before with it, and that I only await her answer, to come myself and fold her again in my arms.

WAITWELL: I think you do well to prepare them for your arrival in this way.

SIR WILLIAM: I make sure of her intentions by this means, and give her the opportunity of freeing herself from any shame or sorrow which repentance might cause her, before she speaks verbally with me. In a letter it will cost her less embarrassment, and me, perhaps, fewer tears.

WAITWELL: But may I ask, Sir, what you have resolved upon with regard to Mellefont?

SIR WILLIAM: Ah, Waitwell, if I could separate him from my daughter's lover, I should make some very harsh resolve. But as this cannot be, you see, he is saved from my anger. I myself am most to blame in this misfortune. But for me Sara would never have made the acquaintance of this dangerous man. I admitted him freely into my house on account of an obligation under which I believed myself to be to him. It was natural that the attention which in gratitude I paid him, should win for him the esteem of my daughter. And it was just as natural, that a man of his disposition should suffer himself to be tempted by this esteem to something more. He had been clever enough to transform it into love before I noticed anything at all, and before I had time to inquire into his former life. The evil was done, and I should have done well, if I had forgiven them everything immediately. I wished to be inexorable towards him, and did not consider that I could not be so towards him alone. If I had spared my severity, which came too late, I would at least have prevented their flight. But here I am now, Waitwell! I must fetch them back myself and consider myself happy if only I can make a son of a seducer. For who knows whether he will give up his Marwoods and his other creatures for the sake of a girl who has left nothing for his desires to wish for and who understands so little the bewitching arts of a coquette?

WAITWELL: Well, Sir, it cannot be possible, that a man could be so wicked –

SIR WILLIAM: This doubt, good Waitwell, does honour to your virtue. But why, at the same time, is it true that the limits of human wickedness extend much further still? Go now, and do as I told you! Notice every look as she reads my letter. In this short deviation from virtue she cannot yet have learned the art of dissimulation, to the masks of which only deep-rooted vice can have recourse. You will read her whole soul in her face. Do not let a look escape you which might perhaps indicate indifference to me – disregard of her father. For if you should unhappily discover this, and if she loves me no more, I hope that I shall be able to conquer myself and abandon her to her fate. I hope so, Waitwell. Alas! Would that there were no heart here, to contradict this hope.

Exeunt on different sides.

SCENE TWO

Sara, Mellefont.

Sara's room.

MELLEFONT: I have done wrong, dearest Sara, to leave you in uneasiness about the letter which came just now.

SARA: Oh dear no, Mellefont! I have not been in the least uneasy about it. Could you not love me even though you still had secrets from me?

MELLEFONT: You think, then, that it was a secret?

SARA: But not one which concerns me. And that must suffice for me.

MELLEFONT: You are only too good. Let me nevertheless reveal my secret to you. The letter contained a few lines from a relative of mine, who has heard of my being here. She passes through here on her way to London, and would like to see me. She has begged at the same time to be allowed the honour of paying you a visit.

SARA: It will always be a pleasure to me to make the acquaintance of the respected members of your family. But consider for yourself, whether I can yet appear before one of them without blushing.

MELLEFONT: Without blushing? And for what? For your love to me? It is true, Sara, you could have given your love to a nobler or a richer man. You must be ashamed that you were content to give your heart for another heart only, and that in this exchange you lost sight of your happiness.

SARA: You must know yourself how wrongly you interpret my words.

MELLEFONT: Pardon me, Sara; if my interpretation is wrong, they can have no meaning at all.

SARA: What is the name of your relation?

MELLEFONT: She is – Lady Solmes. You will have heard me mention the name before.

SARA: I don't remember.

MELLEFONT: May I beg you to see her?

SARA: Beg me? You can command me to do so.

MELLEFONT: What a word! No, Sara, she shall not have the happiness of seeing you. She will regret it, but she must submit to it. Sara has her reasons, which I respect without knowing them.

SARA: How hasty you are, Mellefont! I shall expect Lady Solmes, and do my best to show myself worthy of the honour of her visit. Are you content?

MELLEFONT: Ah, Sara! let me confess my ambition. I should like to show you to the whole world! And were I not proud of the possession of such a being, I should reproach myself with not being able to appreciate her value. I will go and bring her to you at once.

    Exit.

SARA: *(Alone)* I hope she will not be one of those proud women, who are so full of their own virtue that they believe themselves above all failings. With one single look of contempt they condemn us, and an equivocal shrug of the shoulders is all the pity we seem to deserve in their eyes.

SCENE THREE

Waitwell, Sara.

BETTY: *(Behind the scenes.)* Just come in here, if you must speak to her yourself!

SARA: *(Looking round.)* Who must speak to me? Whom do I see? Is it possible? You, Waitwell?

WAITWELL: How happy I am to see our young lady again!

SARA: Good God, what do you bring me? I hear already, I hear already; you bring me the news of my father's death! He is gone, the excellent man, the best of fathers! He is gone, and I – I am the miserable creature who has hastened his death.

WAITWELL: Ah, Miss –

SARA: Tell me, quick; tell me, that his last moments were not embittered by the thought of me; that he had forgotten me; that he died as peacefully as he used to hope to die in my arms; that he did not remember me even in his last prayers –

WAITWELL: Pray do not torment yourself with such false notions! Your father is still alive! He is still alive, honest Sir William!

SARA: Is he still alive? Is it true? Is he still alive? May he live a long while yet, and live happily! Oh, would that God

would add the half of my years to his life! Half! How
ungrateful should I be, if I were not willing to buy
even a few moments for him with all the years that may
yet be mine! But tell me at least, Waitwell, that it is
not hard for him to live without me; that it was easy
for him to renounce a daughter who could so easily
renounce her virtue, that he is angry with me for my
flight, but not grieved; that he curses me, but does not
mourn for me.

WAITWELL: Ah! Sir William is still the same fond father, as his
Sara is still the same fond daughter that she was.

SARA: What do you say? You are a messenger of evil, of the
most dreadful of all the evils which my imagination has
ever pictured to me! He is still the same fond father?
Then he loves me still? And he must mourn for me,
then! No no, he does not do so; he cannot do so? Do
you not see how infinitely each sigh which he wasted
on me would magnify my crime? Would not the justice
of heaven have to charge me with every tear which I
forced from him, as if with each one I repeated my vice
and my ingratitude? I grow chill at the thought. I cause
him tears? Tears? And they are other tears than tears of
joy? Contradict me, Waitwell! At most he has felt some
slight stirring of the blood on my account; some
transitory emotion, calmed by a slight effort of reason.
He did not go so far as to shed tears, surely not to shed
tears, Waitwell?

WAITWELL: *(Wiping his eyes.)* No, Miss, he did not go so far as
that.

SARA: Alas! your lips say no, and your eyes say yes.

WAITWELL: Take this letter, Miss, it is from him himself –

SARA: From whom? From my father? To me?

WAITWELL: Yes, take it! You can learn more from it, than I am
able to say. He ought to have given this to another to
do, not to me. I promised myself pleasure from it; but
you turn my joy into sadness.

SARA: Give it me, honest Waitwell! But no! I will not take it
before you tell me what it contains.

WAITWELL: What can it contain? Love and forgiveness.

SARA: Love? Forgiveness?

WAITWELL: And perhaps a real regret, that he used the rights of a father's power against a child, who should only have the privileges of a father's kindness.

SARA: Then keep your cruel letter.

WAITWELL: Cruel? Have no fear. Full liberty is granted you over your heart and hand.

SARA: And it is just this which I fear. To grieve a father such as he, this I have had the courage to do. But to see him forced by this very grief - by his love which I have forfeited, to look with leniency on all the wrong into which an unfortunate passion has led me; this, Waitwell, I could not bear. If his letter contained all the hard and angry words which an exasperated father can utter in such a case, I should read it - with a shudder it is true - but still I should be able to read it. I should be able to produce a shadow of defence against his wrath, to make him by this defence if possible more angry still. My consolation then would be this - that melancholy grief could have no place with violent wrath and that the latter would transform itself finally into bitter contempt. And we grieve no more for one whom we despise. My father would have grown calm again, and I would not have to reproach myself with having made him unhappy for ever.

WAITWELL: Alas, Miss! You will have to reproach yourself still less for this if you now accept his love again, which wishes only to forget everything.

SARA: You are mistaken, Waitwell! His yearning for me misleads him, perhaps, to give his consent to everything. But no sooner would this desire be appeased a little, than he would feel ashamed before himself of his weakness. Sullen anger would take possession of him, and he would never be able to look at me without silently accusing me of all that I had dared to exact from him. Yes, if it were in my power to spare him his bitterest grief, when on my account he is laying the greatest restraint upon himself: if at a moment when he would grant me everything I could sacrifice all to him; then it would be quite a different matter. I would take the letter from your hands with pleasure, would admire in it the strength of the fatherly love, and, not to abuse this love, I would throw myself at his feet a repentant and obedient daughter. But can I do that? I shall be obliged to make use of his permission, regardless of the price this permission has cost him. And then, when I feel most happy, it will suddenly occur to me that he only outwardly appears to share my happiness and that inwardly he is sighing – in short, that he has made me happy by the renunciation of his own happiness. And to wish to be happy in this way, – do you expect that of me, Waitwell?

WAITWELL: I truly do not know what answer to give to that.

SARA: There is no answer to it. So take your letter back! If my father must be unhappy through me, I will myself remain unhappy also. To be quite alone in unhappiness is that for which I now pray Heaven every hour, but to be quite alone in my happiness – of that I will not hear.

WAITWELL: (Aside) I really think I shall have to employ deception with this good child to get her to read the letter.

SARA: What are you saying to yourself?

WAITWELL: I was saying to myself that the idea I had hit on to get you to read this letter all the quicker was a very clumsy one.

SARA: How so?

WAITWELL: I could not look far enough. Of course you see more deeply into things than such as I. I did not wish to frighten you; the letter is perhaps only too hard; and when I said that it contained nothing but love and forgiveness, I ought to have said that I wished it might not contain anything else.

SARA: Is that true? Give it me then! I will read it. If one has been unfortunate enough to deserve the anger of one's father, one should at least have enough respect for it to submit to the expression of it on his part. To try to

frustrate it means to heap contempt on insult. I shall
feel his anger in all its strength. You see I tremble
already. But I must tremble; and I will rather tremble
than weep. *(Opens the letter.)* Now it is opened! I sink!
But what do I see? *(She reads.)* "My only, dearest
daughter" – ah, you old deceiver, is that the language
of an angry father? Go, I shall read no more –

WAITRESS: Ah, Miss! You will pardon an old servant! Yes, truly, I
believe it is the first time in my life that I have
intentionally deceived anyone. He who deceives once,
Miss, and deceives for so good a purpose, is surely no
old deceiver on that account. That touches me deeply,
Miss! I know well that the good intention does not
always excuse one; but what else could I do? To return
his letter unread to such a good father? That certainly I
cannot do! Sooner will I walk as far as my old legs will
carry me, and never again come into his presence.

SARA: What? You too will leave him?

WAITWELL: Shall I not be obliged to do so if you do not read the
letter? Read it, pray! Do not grudge a good result to
the first deceit with which I have to reproach myself.
You will forget it the sooner, and I shall the sooner be
able to forgive myself. I am a common, simple man,
who must not question the reasons why you cannot and
will not read the letter. Whether they are true, I know
not, but at any rate they do not appear to me to be
natural. I should think thus, Miss: a father, I should
think, is after all a father; and a child may err for once,
and remain a good child in spite of it. If the father
pardons the error, the child may behave again in such a
manner that the father may not even think of it any
more. For who likes to remember what he would rather
had never happened? It seems, Miss, as if you thought only
of your error, and believed you atoned sufficiently in
exaggerating it in your imagination and tormenting
yourself with these exaggerated ideas. But, I should think,
you ought also to consider how you could make up for what
has happened. And how will you make up for it, if you
deprive yourself of every opportunity of doing so. Can it be
hard for you to take the second step, when such a good
father has already taken the first?

SARA: What daggers pierce my heart in your simple words!
            That he has to take the first step is just what I cannot
            bear. And, besides, is it only the first step which he
            takes? He must do all! I cannot take a single one to
            meet him. As far as I have gone from him, so far must
            he descend to me. If he pardons me, he must pardon
            the whole crime, and in addition must bear the
            consequences of it continually before his eyes. Can one
            demand that from a father?

WAITWELL: I do not know, Miss, whether I understand this quite
            right. But it seems to me, you mean to say that he
            would have to forgive you too much, and as this could
            not but be very difficult to him, you make a scruple of
            accepting his forgiveness. If you mean that, tell me,
            pray, is not forgiving a great happiness to a kind heart?
            I have not been so fortunate in my life as to have felt
            this happiness often. But I still remember with pleasure
            the few instances when I have felt it. I felt something
            so sweet, something so tranquillising, something so
            divine, that I could not help thinking of the great
            insurpassable blessedness of God, whose preservation of
            miserable mankind is a perpetual forgiveness. I wished
            that I could be forgiving continually, and was ashamed
            that I had only such trifles to pardon. To forgive real
            painful insults, deadly offences, I said to myself, must
            be a bliss in which the whole soul melts. And now,
            Miss, will you grudge your father such bliss?

SARA: Ah! Go on, Waitwell, go on!

WAITWELL: I know well there are people who accept nothing less
            willingly than forgiveness, and that because they have
            never learned to grant it. They are proud, unbending
            people, who will on no account confess that they have
            done wrong. But you do not belong to this kind, Miss!
            You have the most loving and tender of hearts that the
            best of your sex can have. You confess your fault too.
            Where then is the difficulty? But pardon me, Miss! I
            am an old chatterer, and ought to have seen at once
            that your refusal is only a praiseworthy solicitude, only
            a virtuous timidity. People who can accept a great
            benefit immediately without any hesitation are seldom
            worthy of it. Those who deserve it most have always

the greatest mistrust of themselves. Yet mistrust must
not be pushed beyond limits!

SARA: Dear old father! I believe you have persuaded me.

WAITWELL: If I have been so fortunate as that it must have been a
            good spirit that has helped me to plead. But no, Miss,
            my words have done no more than given you time to
            reflect and to recover from the bewilderment of joy.
            You will read the letter now, will you not? Oh, read it
            at once!

SARA: I will do so, Waitwell! What regrets, what pain shall I
            feel!

WAITWELL: Pain, Miss! But pleasant pain.

SARA: Be silent!

            Begins reading to herself.

WAITWELL: *(Aside)* Oh! If he could see her himself!

SARA: *(After reading a few moments.)* Ah, Waitwell, what a
            father! He calls my flight "an absence." How much
            more culpable it becomes through this gentle word!
            (Continues reading and interrupts herself again.) Listen!
            he flatters himself I shall love him still. He flatters
            himself! He begs me – he begs me? A father begs his
            daughter? His culpable daughter? And what does he beg
            then? He begs me to forget his over-hasty severity, and
            not to punish himself any longer with my absence.
            Over-hasty severity! To punish! More still! Now he
            thanks me even, and thanks me that I have given him
            an opportunity of learning the whole extent of paternal
            love. Unhappy opportunity! Would that he also said it
            had shown him at the same time the extent of filial
            disobedience. No, he does not say it! He does not
            mention my crime with one single word. *(Continues
            reading.)* He will come himself and fetch his children.
            His children, Waitwell! That surpasses everything! Have
            I read it rightly? *(Reads again to herself.)* I am
            overcome! He says, that he without whom he could not
            possess a daughter deserves but too well to be his son.
            Oh that he had never had this unfortunate daughter!
            Go, Waitwell, leave me alone! He wants an answer, and
            I will write it at once. Come again in an hour! I thank

you meanwhile for your trouble. You are an honest
man. Few servants are the friends of their masters!

WAITWELL :   Do not make me blush, Miss! If all masters were like
Sir William, servants would be monsters, if they would
not give their lives for them.

Exit.

SCENE FOUR

SARA :   *(Sits down to write.)* If they had told me a year ago that
I should have to answer such a letter! And under such
circumstances! Yes, I have the pen in my hand. But do
I know yet what I shall write? What I think; what I
feel. And what then does one think when a thousand
thoughts cross each other in one moment? And what
does one feel, when the heart is in a stupor from a
thousand feelings. But I must write! I do not guide the
pen for the first time. After assisting me in so many a
little act of politeness and friendship, should its help
fail me at the most important office? *(She pauses, and
then writes a few lines.)* It shall commence so? A very
cold beginning! And shall I then begin with his love? I
must begin with my crime. *(She scratches it out and
writes again.)* I must be on my guard not to express
myself too leniently. Shame may be in its place
anywhere else, but not in the confession of our faults. I
need not fear falling into exaggeration, even though I
employ the most dreadful terms. Ah, am I to be
interrupted now?

SCENE FIVE

Marwood, Mellefont, Sara.

MELLEFONT :   Dearest Sara, I have the honour of introducing Lady
Solmes to you; she is one of the members of my family
to whom I feel myself most indebted.

MARWOOD :   I must beg your pardon, Madam, for taking the liberty
of convincing myself with my own eyes of the
happiness of a cousin, for whom I should wish the

most perfect of women if the first moment had not at
once convinced me, that he has found her already in
you.

SARA: Your ladyship does me too much honour! Such a
              compliment would have made me blush at any time,
              but now I would almost take it as concealed reproach,
              if I did not think that Lady Solmes is much too
              generous to let her superiority in virtue and wisdom be
              felt by an unhappy girl.

MARWOOD: *(Coldly)* I should be inconsolable if you attributed to
              me any but the most friendly feelings towards you.
              (Aside) She is good-looking.

MELLEFONT: Would it be possible Madam, to remain indifferent to
              such beauty, such modesty? People say, it is true, that
              one charming woman rarely does another one justice,
              but this is to be taken only of those who are over-vain
              of their superiority, and on the other hand of those
              who are not conscious of possessing any superiority.
              How far are you both removed from this. *(To
              Marwood, who stands in deep thought.)* Is it not true,
              Madam, that my love has been anything but partial? Is
              it not true, that though I have said much to you in
              praise of my Sara, I have not said nearly so much as
              you yourself see? But why so thoughtful? *(Aside to her.)*
              You forget whom you represent.

MARWOOD: May I say it? The admiration of your dear young lady
              led me to the contemplation of her fate. It touched me,
              that she should not enjoy the fruits of her love in her
              native land. I recollected that she had to leave a father,
              and a very affectionate father as I have been told, in
              order to become yours; and I could not but wish for
              her reconciliation with him.

SARA: Ah, Madam! how much am I indebted to you for this
              wish. It encourages me to tell you the whole of my
              happiness. You cannot yet know, Mellefont, that this
              wish was granted before Lady Solmes had the kindness
              to wish it.

MELLEFONT: How do you mean, Sara?

MARWOOD: *(Aside)* How am I to interpret that?

SARA: I have just received a letter from my father. Waitwell
                brought it to me. Ah, Mellefont, such a letter!

MELLEFONT: Quick, relieve me from my uncertainty. What have I to
                fear? What have I to hope? Is he still the father from
                whom we fled? And if he is, will Sara be the daughter
                who loves me so tenderly as to fly again? Alas, had I
                but done as you wished, dearest Sara, we should now
                be united by a bond which no caprice could dissolve. I
                feel now all the misfortune which the discovery of our
                abode may bring upon me. – He will come and tear
                you out of my arms. How I hate the contemptible
                being who has betrayed us to him! *(With an angry
                glance at Marwood.)*

SARA: Dearest Mellefont, how flattering to me is this
                uneasiness! And how happy are we both in that it is
                unnecessary. Read his letter! *(To Marwood, whilst
                Mellefont reads the letter.)* He will be astonished at the
                love of my father. Of *my* father? Ah, he is *his* now too.

MARWOOD: *(Perplexed)* Is it possible?

SARA: Yes, Madam, you have good cause to be surprised at
                this change. He forgives us everything; we shall now
                love each other before his eyes; he allows it, he
                commands it. How has this kindness gone to my very
                soul! Well, Mellefont? *(Who returns the letter to her.)*
                You are silent? Oh no, this tear which steals from your
                eye says far more than your lips could say.

MARWOOD: *(Aside)* How I have injured my own cause. Imprudent
                woman that I was!

SARA: Oh, let me kiss this tear from your cheek.

MELLEFONT: Ah, Sara, why was it our fate to grieve such a godlike
                man? Yes, a godlike man, for what is more godlike than
                to forgive? Could we only have imagined such a happy
                issue possible, we should not now owe it to such violent
                means, we should owe it to our entreaties alone. What
                happiness is in store for me! But how painful also will
                be the conviction, that I am so unworthy of this
                happiness!

MARWOOD: *(Aside)* And I must be present to hear this.

SARA: How perfectly you justify my love by such thoughts.

MARWOOD: *(Aside)* What restraint must I put on myself!

SARA: You too, Madam, must read my father's letter. You
             seem to take too great an interest in our fate to be
             indifferent to its contents.

MARWOOD: Indifference?

             Takes letter.

SARA: But, Madam, you still seem very thoughtful, very sad –

MARWOOD: Thoughtful, but not sad!

MELLEFONT: *(Aside)* Heavens! If she should betray herself!

SARA: And why then thoughtful?

MARWOOD: I tremble for you both. Could not this unforeseen
             kindness of your father be a dissimulation? An artifice?

SARA: Assuredly not, Madam, assuredly not. Only read and
             you will admit it yourself. Dissimulation is always
             cold, it is not capable of such tender words. *(Marwood
             reads.)* Do not grow suspicious, Mellefont, I beg. I
             pledge myself that my father cannot condescend to an
             artifice. He says nothing which he does not think,
             falseness is a vice unknown to him.

MELLEFONT: Oh, of that I am thoroughly convinced, dearest Sara!
             You must pardon Lady Solmes for this suspicion, since
             she does not know the man whom it concerns.

SARA: *(Whilst Marwood returns the letter to her.)* What do I
             see, my lady? You are pale! You tremble! What is the
             matter with you?

MELLEFONT: *(Aside)* What anxiety I suffer! Why did I bring her
             here?

MARWOOD: It is nothing but a slight dizziness, which will pass
             over. The night air on my journey must have disagreed
             with me.

MELLEFONT: You frighten me! Would you not like to go into the air?
             You will recover sooner than in a close room.

MARWOOD: If you think so, give me your arm!

SARA:	I will accompany your ladyship!
MARWOOD:	I beg you will not trouble to do so! My faintness will pass over immediately.
SARA:	I hope then, to see you again soon.
MARWOOD:	If you permit me.

Mellefont conducts her out.

SARA:	(*Alone*) Poor thing! She does not seem exactly the most friendly of people; but yet she does not appear to be either proud or ill-tempered. I am alone again. Can I employ the few moments, while I remain so, better than by finishing my answer?

Is about to sit down to write.

SCENE SIX

Betty, Sara.

BETTY:	That was indeed a very short visit.
SARA:	Yes, Betty! It was Lady Solmes, a relation of my Mellefont. She was suddenly taken faint. Where is she now?
BETTY:	Mellefont has accompanied her to the door.
SARA:	She is gone again, then?
BETTY:	I suppose so. But the more I look at you – you must forgive my freedom, Miss – the more you seem to me to be altered. There is something calm, something contented in your looks. Either Lady Solmes must have been a very pleasant visitor, or the old man a very pleasant messenger.
SARA:	The latter, Betty, the latter! He came from my father. What a tender letter I have for you to read! Your kind heart has often wept with me, now it shall rejoice with me, too. I shall be happy again, and be able to reward you for your good services.
BETTY:	What services could I render you in nine short weeks?

SARA: You could not have done more for me in all the rest of my life, than in these nine weeks. They are over! But come now with me, Betty. As Mellefont is probably alone again, I must speak to him. It just occurs to me that it would be well if he wrote at the same time to my father, to whom an expression of gratitude from him could hardly come unexpectedly. Come!

   Exeunt.

SCENE SEVEN

The drawing-room.

Sir William Sampson, Waitwell.

SIR WILLIAM: What balm you have poured on my wounded heart with your words, Waitwell! I live again, and the prospect of her return seems to carry me as far back to my youth as her flight had brought me nearer to my grave. She loves me still? What more do I wish! Go back to her soon, Waitwell! I am impatient for the moment when I shall fold her again in these arms, which I had stretched out so longingly to death! How welcome would it have been to me in the moments of my grief! And how terrible will it be to me in my new happiness! An old man, no doubt, is to be blamed for drawing the bonds so tight again which still unite him to the world. The final separation becomes the more painful. But God who shows Himself so merciful to me now, will also help me to go through this. Would he, I ask, grant me a mercy in order to let it become my ruin in the end? Would He give me back a daughter, that I should have to murmur when He calls me from life? No, no! He gives her back to me that in my last hour I may be anxious about myself alone. Thanks to Thee, Eternal Father! How feeble is the gratitude of mortal lips! But soon, soon I shall be able to thank Him more worthily in an eternity devoted to Him alone!

WAITWELL: How it delights me, Sir, to know you happy again before my death! Believe me, I have suffered almost as much in your grief as you yourself. Almost as much,

for the grief of a father in such a case must be
inexpressible.

SIR WILLIAM: Do not regard yourself as my servant any longer, my
good Waitwell. You have long deserved to enjoy a more
seemly old age. I will give it you, and you shall not be
worse off than I am while I am still in this world. I
will abolish all differences between us; in yonder world,
you well know, it will be done. For this once be the old
servant still, on whom I never relied in vain. Go, and
be sure to bring me her answer, as soon as it is ready.

WAITWELL: I go, Sir! But such an errand is not a service. It is a
reward which you grant me for my services. Yes, truly
it is so.

Exeunt on different sides of the stage.

END OF ACT THREE

ACT FOUR

SCENE ONE

Mellefont's room.

Mellefont, Sara.

MELLEFONT: Yes, dearest Sara, yes! That I will do! That I must do.

SARA: How happy you make me!

MELLEFONT: It is I who must take the whole crime upon myself. I alone am guilty; I alone must ask for forgiveness.

SARA: No, Mellefont, do not take from me the greater share which I have in our error! It is dear to me, however wrong it is, for it must have convinced you that I love my Mellefont above everything in this world. But is it, then really, true, that I may henceforth combine this love with the love of my father? Or am I in a pleasant dream? How I fear it will pass and I shall awaken in my old misery! But no! I am not merely dreaming, I am really happier than I ever dared hope to become; happier than this short life may perhaps allow. But perhaps this beam of happiness appears in the distance, and delusively seems to approach only in order to melt away again into thick darkness, and to leave me suddenly in a night whose whole terror has only become perceptible to me through this short illumination. What forebodings torment me! Are they really forebodings, Mellefont, or are they common feelings, which are inseparable from the expectation of an undeserved happiness, and the fear of losing it? How fast my heart beats, and how wildly it beats. How loud now, how quick! And now how weak, how anxious, how quivering! Now it hurries again, as if these were its last throbbings, which it would fain beat out rapidly. Poor heart!

MELLEFONT: The tumult of your blood, which a sudden surprise cannot fail to cause, will abate, Sara, and your heart will continue its work more calmly. None of its throbs point to aught that is in the future, and we are to

blame – forgive me, dearest Sara! – if we make the
mechanic pressure of our blood into a prophet of evil.
But I will not leave anything undone which you
yourself think good to appease this little storm within
your breast. I will write at once, and I hope that Sir
William will be satisfied with the assurances of my
repentance, with the expressions of my stricken heart,
and my vows of affectionate obedience.

SARA: Sir William? Ah, Mellefont, you must begin now to
accustom yourself to a far more tender name. My
father, your father, Mellefont –

MELLEFONT: Very well, Sara, our kind, our dear father! I was very
young when I last used this sweet name; very young,
when I had to unlearn the equally sweet name of
mother.

SARA: You had to unlearn it, and I – I was never so happy, as
to be able to pronounce it at all. My life was her death!
O God, I was a guiltless matricide! And how much was
wanting – how little, how almost nothing was wanting
to my becoming a parricide too! Not a guiltless, but a
voluntary parricide. And who knows, whether I am not
so already? The years, the days, the moments by which
he is nearer to his end than he would have been
without the grief I have caused him – of those I have
robbed him. However old and weary he may be when
Fate shall permit him to depart, my conscience will yet
be unable to escape the reproach that but for me he
might have lived yet longer. A sad reproach with which
I doubtless should not need to charge myself, if a
loving mother had guided me in my youth. Through
her teaching and her example my heart would – you
look tenderly on me, Mellefont? You are right; a
mother would perhaps have been a tyrant for very love,
and I should not now belong to Mellefont. Why do I
wish then for that, which a wiser Fate denied me out of
kindness? Its dispensations are always best. Let us only
make proper use of that which it gives us; a father who
never yet let me sigh for a mother; a father who will
also teach you to forget the parents you lost so soon.
What a flattering thought. I fall in love with it, and
forget almost, that in my innermost heart there is still

something which refuses to put faith in it. What is this
rebellious something?

MELLEFONT: This something, dearest Sara, as you have already said
yourself, is the natural, timid incapability to realise a
great happiness. Ah, your heart hesitated less to believe
itself unhappy than now, to its own torment, it
hesitates to believe in its own happiness! But as to one
who has become dizzy with quick movement, the
external objects still appear to move round when again
he is sitting still, so the heart which has been violently
agitated cannot suddenly become calm again; there
remains often for a long time, a quivering palpitation
which we must suffer to exhaust itself.

SARA: I believe it, Mellefont, I believe it, because you say it,
because I wish it. But do not let us detain each other
any longer! I will go and finish my letter. And you will
let me read yours, will you not, after I have shown you
mine?

MELLEFONT: Each word shall be submitted to your judgment; except
what I must say in your defence, for I know you do not
think yourself so innocent as you are.

Accompanies Sara to the back of the stage.

SCENE TWO

MELLEFONT: *(After walking up and down several times in thought.)*
What a riddle I am to myself! What shall I think
myself? A fool? Or a knave? Heart, what a villain thou
art! I love the angel, however much of a devil I may
be. I love her! Yes, certainly! Certainly I love her. I feel
I would sacrifice a thousand lives for her, for her who
sacrificed her virtue for me; I would do so – this very
moment without hesitation would I do so. And yet, yet
– I am afraid to say it to myself – and yet – how shall I
explain it? And yet I fear the moment which will make
her mine for ever before the world. It cannot be
avoided now, for her father is reconciled. Nor shall I be
able to put it off for long. The delay has already drawn
down painful reproaches enough upon me. But painful

as they were, they were still more supportable to me
than the melancholy thought of being fettered for life.
But am I not so already? Certainly – and with
pleasure! Certainly I am already her prisoner. What is
it I want, then? At present I am a prisoner, who is
allowed to go about on parole; that is flattering! Why
cannot the matter rest there? Why must I be put in
chains and thus lack even the pitiable shadow of
freedom? In chains? Quite so! Sara Sampson, my
beloved! What bliss lies in these words! Sara Sampson,
my wife! The half of the bliss is gone! And the other
half – will go! Monster that I am! And with such
thoughts shall I write to her father? Yet these are not
my real thoughts, they are fancies! Cursed fancies,
which have become natural to me through my dissolute
life! I will free myself from them, or live no more.

SCENE THREE

Norton, Mellefont.

MELLEFONT: You disturb me, Norton!

NORTON: I beg your pardon, Sir.

             Withdrawing again.

MELLEFONT: No, no! Stay! It is just as well that you should disturb
             me. What do you want?

NORTON: I have heard some very good news from Betty, and
             have come to wish you happiness.

MELLEFONT: On the reconciliation with her father, I suppose you
             mean? I thank you.

NORTON: So Heaven still means to make you happy.

MELLEFONT: If it means to do so – you see, Norton, I am just
             towards myself – it certainly does not mean it for my
             sake.

NORTON: No, no; if you feel that, then it will be for your sake
             also.

MELLEFONT: For my Sara's sake alone. If its vengeance, already
             armed, could spare the whole of a sinful city for the

sake of a few just men, surely it can also bear with a
sinner, when a soul in which it finds delight, is the
sharer of his fate.

NORTON: You speak with earnestness and feeling. But does not
joy express itself differently from this?

MELLEFONT: Joy, Norton? *(Looking sharply at him.)* For me it is
gone now for ever.

NORTON: May I speak candidly?

MELLEFONT: You may.

NORTON: The reproach which I had to hear this morning of
having made myself a participator in your crimes,
because I had been silent about them, may excuse me,
if I am less silent henceforth.

MELLEFONT: Only do not forget who you are!

NORTON: I will not forget that I am a servant, and a servant,
alas, who might be something better, if he had lived for
it. I am your servant, it is true, but not so far as to
wish to be damned along with you.

MELLEFONT: With me? And why do you say that now?

NORTON: Because I am not a little astonished to find you
different from what I expected.

MELLEFONT: Will you not inform me what you expected?

NORTON: To find you all delight

MELLEFONT: It is only the common herd who are beside themselves
immediately when luck smiles on them for once.

NORTON: Perhaps, because the common herd still have the
feelings which among greater people are corrupted and
weakened by a thousand unnatural notions. But there is
something besides moderation to be read in your face –
coldness, irresolution, disinclination.

MELLEFONT: And if so? Have you forgotten who is here besides
Sara? The presence of Marwood –

NORTON: Could make you anxious, I daresay, but not despondent.
Something else troubles you. And I shall be glad to be
mistaken in thinking you would rather that the father

were not yet reconciled. The prospect of a position
which so little suits your way of thinking –

MELLEFONT: Norton, Norton! Either you must have been, or still
must be, a dreadful villain, that you can thus guess my
thoughts. Since you have hit the nail upon the head, I
will not deny it. It is true – so certain as it is that I
shall love my Sara for ever so little does it please me,
that I *must* – *must* love her for ever! But do not fear; I
shall conquer this foolish fancy. Or do you think that it
is no fancy? Who bids me look at marriage as
compulsion? I certainly do not wish to be freer than
she will permit me to be.

NORTON: These reflections are all very well. But Marwood will
come to the aid of your old prejudices, and I fear, I
fear –

MELLEFONT: That which will never happen! You see her go back
this very evening to London. And as I have confessed
my most secret – folly we will call it for the present – I
must not conceal from you either, that I have put
Marwood into such a fright that she will obey the
slightest hint from me.

NORTON: That sounds incredible to me.

MELLEFONT: Look! I snatched this murderous steel from her hand
(*Showing the dagger which he has taken from Marwood.*)
when in a fearful rage she was on the point of stabbing
me to the heart with it. Will you believe now, that I
offered her a stout resistance? At first she well nigh
succeeded in throwing her noose around my neck again.
The traitress! – She has Arabella with her.

NORTON: Arabella?

MELLEFONT: I have not yet been able to fathom by what cunning
she got the child back into her hands again. Enough,
the result did not fall out as she no doubt had
expected.

NORTON: Allow me to rejoice at your firmness, and to consider
your reformation half assured. Yet – as you wish me to
know all – what business had she here under the name
of Lady Solmes?

MELLEFONT: She wanted of all things to see her rival. I granted her wish partly from kindness, partly from rashness, partly from the desire to humiliate her by the sight of the best of her sex. You shake your head, Norton?

NORTON: I should not have risked that.

MELLEFONT: Risked? I did not risk anything more, after all, than what I should have had to risk if I had refused her. She would have tried to obtain admittance as Marwood; and the worst that can be expected from her incognito visit is not worse than that.

NORTON: Thank Heaven that it went off so quietly.

MELLEFONT: It is not quite over yet, Norton. A slight indisposition came over her and compelled her to go away without taking leave. She wants to come again. Let her do so! The wasp which has lost its sting *(Pointing to the dagger.)* can do nothing worse than buzz. But buzzing too shall cost her dear, if she grows too troublesome with it. Do I not hear somebody coming? Leave me if it should be she. It is she. Go!

Exit Norton.

SCENE FOUR

Mellefont, Marwood.

MARWOOD: No doubt you are little pleased to see me again.

MELLEFONT: I am very pleased, Marwood, to see that your indisposition has had no further consequences. You are better, I hope?

MARWOOD: So, so.

MELLEFONT: You have not done well, then, to trouble to come here again.

MARWOOD: I thank you, Mellefont, if you say this out of kindness to me; and I do not take it amiss, if you have another meaning in it.

MELLEFONT: I am pleased to see you so calm.

MARWOOD: The storm is over. Forget it. I beg you once more.

MELLEFONT: Only remember your promise, Marwood, and I will
              forget everything with pleasure. But if I knew that you
              would not consider it an offence, I should like to ask –

MARWOOD: Ask on, Mellefont! You cannot offend me any more.
              What were you going to ask?

MELLEFONT: How you like my Sara?

MARWOOD: The question is natural. My answer will not seem so
              natural, but it is none the less true for that. I liked her
              very much.

MELLEFONT: Such impartiality delights me. But would it be possible
              for him who knew how to appreciate the charms of a
              Marwood to make a bad choice?

MARWOOD: You ought to have spared me this flattery, Mellefont, if
              it is flattery. It is not in accordance with our intention
              to forget each other.

MELLEFONT: You surely do not wish me to facilitate this intention
              by rudeness? Do not let our separation be of an
              ordinary nature. Let us break with each other as people
              of reason who yield to necessity; without bitterness,
              without anger, and with the preservation of a certain
              degree of respect, as behoves our former intimacy.

MARWOOD: Former intimacy! I do not wish to be reminded of it.
              No more of it. What must be, must, and it matters
              little how. But one word more about Arabella. You will
              not let me have her?

MELLEFONT: No, Marwood!

MARWOOD: It is cruel, since you can no longer be her father, to
              take her mother also from her.

MELLEFONT: I can still be her father, and will be so.

MARWOOD: Prove it, then, now!

MELLEFONT: How?

MARWOOD: Permit Arabella to have the riches which I have in
              keeping for you, as her father's inheritance. As to her
              mother's inheritance I wish I could leave her a better
              one than the shame of having been borne by me.

MELLEFONT: Do not speak so! I shall provide for Arabella without
embarrassing her mother's property. If she wishes
to forget me, she must begin by forgetting that she
possesses anything from me. I have obligations towards
her, and I shall never forget that really – though
against her will – she has promoted my happiness. Yes,
Marwood, in all seriousness I thank you for betraying
our retreat to a father whose ignorance of it alone
prevented him from receiving us again.

MARWOOD: Do not torture me with gratitude which I never wished
to deserve. Sir William is too good an old fool; he must
think differently from what I should have thought in his
place. I should have forgiven my daughter, but as to
her seducer I should have –

MELLEFONT: Marwood!

MARWOOD: True; you yourself are the seducer! I am silent. Shall I
be presently allowed to pay my farewell visit to Miss
Sampson?

MELLEFONT: Sara could not be offended, even if you left without
seeing her again.

MARWOOD: Mellefont, I do not like playing my part by halves, and
I have no wish to be taken, even under an assumed
name, for a woman without breeding.

MELLEFONT: If you care for your own peace of mind you ought to
avoid seeing a person again who must awaken certain
thoughts in you which –

MARWOOD: *(Smiling disdainfully.)* You have a better opinion of
yourself than of me. But even if you believed that I
should be inconsolable on your account, you ought at
least to believe it in silence. – Miss Sampson would
awaken certain thoughts in me? Certain thoughts! Oh,
yes; but none more certain than this – that the best girl
can often love the most worthless man.

MELLEFONT: Charming, Marwood, perfectly charming. Now you are
as I have long wished to see you; although I could
almost have wished, as I told you before, that we could
have retained some respect for each other. But this may
perhaps come still when once your fermenting heart has

cooled down. Excuse me for a moment. I will fetch
Miss Sampson to see you.

Exit.

SCENE FIVE

MARWOOD: *(Looking round.)* Am I alone? Can I take breath again
unobserved, and let the muscles of my face relax into
their natural position? I must just for a moment be the
true Marwood in all my features to be able again to
bear the restraint of dissimulation! How I hate thee,
base dissimulation! Not because I love sincerity, but
because thou art the most pitiable refuge of powerless
revenge. I certainly would not condescend to thee, if a
tyrant would lend me his power or Heaven its
thunderbolt. – Yet, if thou only servest my end! The
beginning is promising, and Mellefont seems disposed
to grow more confident. If my device succeeds and I can
speak alone with his Sara; then – yes, then, it is still
very uncertain whether it will be of any use to me. The
truths about Mellefont will perhaps be no novelty to
her; and the calumnies she will perhaps not believe,
and the threats, perhaps, despise. But yet she shall hear
truths, calumnies and threats. It would be bad, if they
did not leave any sting at all in her mind. Silence; they
are coming. I am no longer Marwood, I am a worthless
outcast, who tries by little artful tricks to turn aside her
shame – a bruised worm, which turns and fain would
wound at least the heel of him who trod upon it.

SCENE SIX

Sara, Mellefont, Marwood.

SARA: I am happy, Madam, that my uneasiness on your
account has been unnecessary.

MARWOOD: I thank you! The attack was so insignificant that it need
not have made you uneasy.

MELLEFONT: Lady Solmes wishes to take leave of you, dearest Sara!

SARA: So soon, Madam?

MARWOOD: I cannot go soon enough for those who desire my presence in London.

MELLEFONT: You surely are not going to leave today?

MARWOOD: Tomorrow morning, first thing.

MELLEFONT: Tomorrow morning, first thing? I thought today.

SARA: Our acquaintance, Madam, commences hurriedly. I hope to be honoured with a more intimate intercourse with you at some future time.

MARWOOD: I solicit your friendship, Miss Sampson.

MELLEFONT: I pledge myself, dearest Sara, that this desire of Lady Solmes is sincere, although I must tell you beforehand that you will certainly not see each other again for a long time. Lady Solmes will very rarely be able to live where we are.

MARWOOD: *(Aside)* How subtle!

SARA: That is to deprive me of a very pleasant anticipation, Mellefont!

MARWOOD: I shall be the greatest loser!

MELLEFONT: But in reality, Madam, do you not start before tomorrow morning?

MARWOOD: It may be sooner! *(Aside)* No one comes.

MELLEFONT: We do not wish to remain much longer here either. It will be well, will it not, Sara, to follow our answer without delay? Sir William cannot be displeased with our haste.

SCENE SEVEN

Betty, Mellefont, Sara, Marwood.

MELLEFONT: What is it, Betty?

BETTY: Somebody wishes to speak with you immediately.

MARWOOD: *(Aside)* Ha! Now all depends on whether –

MELLEFONT: Me? Immediately? I will come at once. Madam, is it
                agreeable to you to shorten your visit?

SARA: Why so, Mellefont? Lady Solmes will be so kind as to
                wait for your return.

MARWOOD: Pardon me; I know my cousin Mellefont, and prefer to
                depart with him.

BETTY: The stranger, sir – he wishes only to say a word to you.
                He says, that he has not a moment to lose.

MELLEFONT: Go, please! I will be with him directly. I expect it will
                be some news at last about the agreement which I
                mentioned to you.

            Exit Betty.

MARWOOD: *(Aside)* A good conjecture!

MELLEFONT: But still, Madam –

MARWOOD: If you order it, then, I must bid you –

SARA: Oh no, Mellefont; I am sure you will not grudge me
                the pleasure of entertaining Lady Solmes during your
                absence?

MELLEFONT: You wish it, Sara?

SARA: Do not stay now, dearest Mellefont, but come back
                again soon! And come with a more joyful face, I will
                wish! You doubtless expect an unpleasant answer.
                Don't let this disturb you. I am more desirous to see
                whether after all you can gracefully prefer me to an
                inheritance, than I am to know that you are in
                possession of one.

MELLEFONT: I obey. *(In a warning tone.)* I shall be sure to come
                back in a moment, Madam.

MARWOOD: *(Aside)* Lucky so far.

            Exit Mellefont.

SCENE EIGHT

Sara, Marwood.

SARA: My good Mellefont sometimes gives his polite phrases
           quite a wrong accent. Do not you think so too,
           Madam?

MARWOOD: I am no doubt too much accustomed to his way already
           to notice anything of that sort.

SARA: Will you not take a seat, Madam?

MARWOOD: If you desire it. *(Aside, whilst they are seating
           themselves.)* I must not let this moment slip by unused.

SARA: Tell me! Shall I not be the most enviable of women
           with my Mellefont?

MARWOOD: If Mellefont knows how to appreciate his happiness,
           Miss Sampson will make him the most enviable of men.
           But –

SARA: A "but," and then a pause, Madam –

MARWOOD: I am frank, Miss Sampson.

SARA: And for this reason infinitely more to be esteemed.

MARWOOD: Frank – not seldom imprudently so. My "but" is a
           proof of it. A very imprudent "but."

SARA: I do not think that my Lady Solmes can wish through
           this evasion to make me more uneasy. It must be a
           cruel mercy that only rouses suspicions of an evil which
           it might disclose.

MARWOOD: Not at all, Miss Sampson! You attach far too much
           importance to my "but". Mellefont is a relation of
           mine –

SARA: Then all the more important is the slightest charge
           which you have to make against him.

MARWOOD: But even were Mellefont my brother, I must tell you,
           that I should unhesitatingly side with one of my own
           sex against him, if I perceived that he did not act quite
           honestly towards her. We women ought properly to

consider every insult shown to one of us as an insult to
the whole sex, and to make it a common affair, in
which even the sister and mother of the guilty one
ought not to hesitate to share.

SARA: This remark –

MARWOOD: Has already been my guide now and then in doubtful
           cases.

SARA: And promises me – I tremble.

MARWOOD: No, Miss Sampson, if you mean to tremble, let us
           speak of something else –

SARA: Cruel woman!

MARWOOD: I am sorry to be misunderstood. I at least, if I place
           myself in imagination in Miss Sampson's position,
           would regard as a favour any more exact information
           which one might give me about the man with whose
           fate I was about to unite my own for ever.

SARA: What do you wish, Madam? Do I not know my
           Mellefont already? Believe me I know him, as I do my
           own soul. I know that he loves me –

MARWOOD: And others –

SARA: *Has* loved others. That I know also. Was he to love me,
           before he knew anything about me? Can I ask to be the
           only one who has had charm enough to attract him?
           Must I not confess it to myself, that I have striven to
           please him? Is he not so lovable, that he must have
           awakened this endeavour in many a breast? And isn't it
           but natural, if several have been successful in their
           endeavour?

MARWOOD: You defend him with just the same ardour and almost
           the same words with which I have often defended him
           already. It is no crime to have loved; much less still is
           it a crime to have been loved. But fickleness is a crime.

SARA: Not always; for often, I believe it is rendered excusable
           by the objects of one's love, which seldom deserve to
           be loved for ever.

MARWOOD: Miss Sampson's doctrine of morals does not seem to be
           of the strictest.

SARA: It is true; the one by which I judge those who
            themselves confess that they have taken to bad ways is
            not of the strictest. Nor should it be so. For here it is
            not a question of fixing the limits which virtue marks
            out for love, but merely of excusing the human
            weakness that has not remained within those limits and
            of judging the consequences arising therefrom by the
            rules of wisdom. If, for example, a Mellefont loves a
            Marwood and eventually abandons her; this
            abandonment is very praiseworthy in comparison with
            the love itself. It would be a misfortune if he had to
            love a vicious person for ever because he once had
            loved her.

MARWOOD: But do you know this Marwood, whom you so
            confidently call a vicious person?

SARA: I know her from Mellefont's description.

MARWOOD: Mellefont's? Has it never occurred to you then that
            Mellefont must be a very invalid witness in his own
            affairs?

SARA: I see now, Madam, that you wish to put me to the test.
            Mellefont will smile, when you repeat to him how
            earnestly I have defended him.

MARWOOD: I beg your pardon, Miss Sampson, Mellefont must not
            hear anything about this conversation. You are of too
            noble a mind to wish out of gratitude for a well-meant
            warning to estrange from him a relation who speaks
            against him only because she looks upon his unworthy
            behaviour towards more than one of the most amiable
            of her sex as if she herself had suffered from it.

SARA: I do not wish to estrange anyone, and would that
            others wished it as little as I do.

MARWOOD: Shall I tell you the story of Marwood in a few words?

SARA: I do not know. But still – yes, Madam! But under the
            condition that you stop as soon as Mellefont returns.
            He might think that I had inquired about it myself;
            and I should not like him to think me capable of a
            curiosity so prejudicial to him.

MARWOOD: I should have asked the same caution of Miss Sampson,

if she had not anticipated me. He must not even be
able to suspect that Marwood has been our topic; and
you will be so cautious as to act in accordance with
this. Hear now! Marwood is of good family. She was
a young widow when Mellefont made her acquaintance
at the house of one of her friends. They say, that she
lacked neither beauty, nor the grace without which
beauty would be nothing. Her good name was spotless.
One single thing was wanting. Money. Everything
that she had possessed – and she is said to have had
considerable wealth – she had sacrificed for the
deliverance of a husband from whom she thought it
right to withhold nothing, after she had willed to give
him heart and hand.

SARA: Truly a noble trait of character, which I wish could
            sparkle in a better setting!

MARWOOD: In spite of her want of fortune she was sought by
            persons who wished nothing more than to make her
            happy. Mellefont appeared amongst her rich and
            distinguished admirers. His offer was serious, and the
            abundance in which he promised to place Marwood
            was the least on which he relied. He knew, in their
            earliest intimacy, that he had not to deal with an egoist
            but with a woman of refined feelings, who would have
            preferred to live in a hut with one she loved, than in a
            palace with one for whom she did not care.

SARA: Another trait which I grudge Miss Marwood. Do not
            flatter her any more, pray, Madam, or I might be led
            to pity her at last.

MARWOOD: Mellefont was just about to unite himself with her with
            due solemnity, when he received the news of the death
            of a cousin who left him his entire fortune on the
            condition that he should marry a distant relation. As
            Marwood had refused richer unions for his sake, he
            would not now yield to her in generosity. He intended
            to tell her nothing of this inheritance, until he had
            forfeited it through her. That was generously planned,
            was it not?

SARA: Oh, Madam, who knows better than I, that Mellefont
            possesses the most generous of hearts?

MARWOOD: But what did Marwood do? She heard late one evening, through some friends, of Mellefont's resolution. Mellefont came in the morning to see her, and Marwood was gone.

SARA: Where to? Why?

MARWOOD: He found nothing but a letter from her, in which she told him that he must not expect ever to see her again. She did not deny, though, that she loved him; but for this very reason she could not bring herself to be the cause of an act, of which he must necessarily repent some day. She released him from his promise, and begged him by the consummation of the union, demanded by the will to enter without further delay into the possession of a fortune, which an honourable man could employ for a better purpose than the thoughtless flattery of a woman.

SARA: But, Madam, why do you attribute such noble sentiments to Marwood? Lady Solmes may be capable of such, I daresay, but not Marwood. Certainly not Marwood.

MARWOOD: It is not surprising, that you are prejudiced against her. Mellefont was almost distracted at Marwood's resolution. He sent people in all directions to search for her, and at last found her.

SARA: No doubt, because she wished to be found!

MARWOOD: No bitter jests! They do not become a woman of such gentle disposition. I say, he found her; and found her inexorable. She would not accept his hand on any account, and the promise to return to London was all that he could get from her. They agreed to postpone their marriage until his relative, tired of the long delay, should be compelled to propose an arrangement. In the meantime Marwood could not well renounce the daily visits from Mellefont, which for a long time were nothing but the respectful visits of a suitor who has been ordered back within the bounds of friendship. But how impossible is it for a passionate temper not to transgress these bounds. Mellefont possesses everything which can make a man dangerous to us. Nobody can be

more convinced of this than you yourself, Miss
Sampson.

SARA: Alas.

MARWOOD: You sigh! Marwood too has sighed more than once
            over her weakness, and sighs yet.

SARA: Enough, Madam, enough! These words I should think,
            are worse than the bitter jest which you were pleased to
            forbid me.

MARWOOD: Its intention was not to offend you, but only to show
            you the unhappy Marwood in a light in which you
            could most correctly judge her. To be brief – love gave
            Mellefont the rights of a husband; and Mellefont did
            not any longer consider it necessary to have them made
            valid by the law. How happy would Marwood be, if
            she, Mellefont, and Heaven alone knew of her shame!
            How happy if a pitiable daughter did not reveal to the
            whole world that which she would fain be able to hide
            from herself.

SARA: What do you say? A daughter –

MARWOOD: Yes, through the intervention of Sara Sampson, an
            unhappy daughter loses all hope of ever being able to
            name her parents without abhorrence.

SARA: Terrible words! And Mellefont has concealed this from
            me? Am I to believe it, Madam?

MARWOOD: You may assuredly believe that Mellefont has perhaps
            concealed still more from you.

SARA: Still more? What more could he have concealed from
            me?

MARWOOD: This – that he still loves Marwood.

SARA: You will kill me!

MARWOOD: It is incredible that a love which has lasted more than
            ten years can die away so quickly. It may certainly
            suffer a short eclipse, but nothing but a short one, from
            which it breaks forth again with renewed brightness. I
            could name to you a Miss Oclaff, a Miss Dorcas, a
            Miss Moore, and several others, who one after another
            threatened to alienate from Marwood the man by

whom they eventually saw themselves most cruelly
deceived. There is a certain point beyond which he
cannot go, and as soon as he gets face to face with it he
draws suddenly back. But suppose, Miss Sampson, you
were the one fortunate woman in whose case all
circumstances declared themselves against him; suppose
you succeeded in compelling him to conquer the
disgust of a formal yoke which has now become innate
to him; do you then expect to make sure of his heart in
this way?

SARA: Miserable girl that I am! What must I hear?

MARWOOD: Nothing less than that! He would then hurry back all
the more into the arms of her who had not been so
jealous of his liberty. You would be called his wife and
she would be it.

SARA: Do not torment me longer with such dreadful pictures!
Advise me rather, Madam, I pray you, advise me what
to do. You must know him! You must know by what
means it may still be possible to reconcile him with a
bond without which even the most sincere love remains
an unholy passion.

MARWOOD: That one can catch a bird, I well know; but that one
can render its cage more pleasant than the open field, I
do not know. My advice, therefore, would be that one
should rather not catch it, and should spare oneself the
vexation of the profitless trouble. Content yourself,
young lady, with the pleasure of having seen him very
near your net; and as you can foresee, that he would
certainly tear it if you tempted him in altogether, spare
your net and do not tempt him in.

SARA: I do not know whether I rightly understand your
playful parable –

MARWOOD: If you are vexed with it, you have understood it. In one
word. Your own interest as well as that of another –
wisdom as well as justice, can, and must induce Miss
Sampson to renounce her claims to a man to whom
Marwood has the first and strongest claim. You are still
in such a position with regard to him that you can
withdraw, I will not say with much honour, but still
without public disgrace. A short disappearance with a

lover is a stain, it is true; but still a stain which time effaces. In some years all will be forgotten, and for a rich heiress there are always men to be found, who are not so scrupulous. If Marwood were in such a position, and she needed no husband for her fading charms nor father for her helpless daughter, I am sure she would act more generously towards Miss Sampson than Miss Sampson acts towards her when raising these dishonourable difficulties.

SARA: *(Rising angrily.)* This is too much! Is that the language of a relative of Mellefont's? How shamefully you are betrayed, Mellefont! Now I perceive, Madam, why he was so unwilling to leave you alone with me. He knows already, I daresay, how much one has to fear from your tongue. A poisoned tongue! I speak boldly – for your unseemly talk has continued long enough. How has Marwood been able to enlist such a mediator; a mediator who summons all her ingenuity to force upon me a dazzling romance about her; and employs every art to rouse my suspicion against the loyalty of a man, who is a man but not a monster? Was it only for this that I was told that Marwood boasted of a daughter from him; only for this that I was told of this and that forsaken girl – in order that you might be enabled to hint to me in cruel fashion that I should do well if I gave place to a hardened strumpet.

MARWOOD: Not so passionate, if you please, young lady! A hardened strumpet? You are surely using words whose full meaning you have not considered.

SARA: Does she not appear such, even from Lady Solmes's description? Well, Madam, you are her friend, perhaps her intimate friend. I do not say this as a reproach, for it may well be that it is hardly possible in this world to have virtuous friends only. Yet why should I be so humiliated for the sake of this friendship of yours? If I had had Marwood's experience, I should certainly not have committed the error which places me on such a humiliating level with her. But if I had committed it, I should certainly not have continued in it for ten years. It is one thing to fall into vice from ignorance; and another to grow intimate with it when you know it.

Alas, Madam, if you knew what regret, what remorse, what anxiety my error has cost me! My error, I say, for why shall I be so cruel to myself any longer, and look upon it as a crime? Heaven itself ceases to consider it such; it withdraws my punishment, and gives me back my father. – But I am frightened, Madam; how your features are suddenly transformed! They glow – rage speaks from the fixed eye, and the quivering movement of the mouth. Ah, if I have vexed you, Madam, I beg for pardon! I am a foolish, sensitive creature; what you have said was doubtless not meant so badly. Forget my rashness! How can I pacify you? How can I also gain a friend in you as Marwood has done? Let me, let me entreat you on my knees *(Falling down upon her knees.)* for your friendship, and if I cannot have this, at least for the justice not to place me and Marwood in one and the same rank.

MARWOOD: *(Proudly stepping back and leaving Sara on her knees.)* This position of Sara Sampson is too charming for Marwood to triumph in it unrecognized. In me, Miss Sampson, behold the Marwood with whom on your knees you beg – Marwood herself – not to compare you.

SARA: *(Springing up and drawing back in terror.)* You Marwood? Ha! Now I recognize her – now I recognize the murderous deliverer, to whose dagger a warning dream exposed me. It is she! Away, unhappy Sara! Save me, Mellefont; save your beloved! And thou, sweet voice of my beloved father, call! Where does it call? Whither shall I hasten to it? – here? – there? – Help, Mellefont! Help, Betty! How she approaches me with murderous hand! Help!

Exit.

SCENE NINE

MARWOOD: What does the excitable girl mean? Would that she spake the truth, and that I approached her with murderous hand! I ought to have spared the dagger until now, fool that I was! What delight to be able to stab a rival at one's feet in her voluntary humiliation! What now? I am detected. Mellefont may be here this minute. Shall I fly from him? Shall I await him? I will wait, but not in idleness. Perhaps the cunning of the servant will detain him long enough? I see I am feared. Why do I not follow her then? Why do I not try the last expedient which I can use against her? Threats are pitiable weapons; but despair despises no weapons, however pitiable they may be. A timid girl, who flies stupid and terror-stricken from my mere name, can easily take dreadful words for dreadful deeds. But Mellefont! Mellefont will give her fresh courage, and teach her to scorn my threats. He will! Perhaps he will not! Few things would have been undertaken in this world, if men had always looked to the end. And am I not prepared for the most fatal end? The dagger was for others, the drug is for me! The drug for me! Long carried by me near my heart, it here awaits its sad service; here, where in better times I hid the written flatteries of my lovers – poison for us equally sure if slower. Would it were not destined to rage in my veins only! Would that a faithless one – why do I waste my time in wishing? Away! I must not recover my reason nor she hers. He will dare nothing, who wishes to dare in cold blood!

END OF ACT FOUR

ACT FIVE

SCENE ONE

Sara's room.

Sara (reclining in an armchair), Betty.

BETTY: Do you feel a little better, Miss?

SARA: Better – I wish only that Mellefont would return! You have sent for him, have you not?

BETTY: Norton and the landlord have gone for him.

SARA: Norton is a good fellow, but he is rash. I do not want him by any means to be rude to his master on my account. According to his story, Mellefont is innocent of all this. She follows him; what can he do? She storms, she raves, she tries to murder him. Do you see, Betty, I have exposed him to this danger? Who else but me? And the wicked Marwood at last insisted on seeing me or she would not return to London. Could he refuse her this trifling request? Have not I too often been curious to see Marwood. Mellefont knows well that we are curious creatures. And if I had not insisted myself that she should remain with me until his return, he would have taken her away with him. I should have seen her under a false name, without knowing that I had seen her. And I should perhaps have been pleased with this little deception at some future time. In short, it is all my fault. Well, well, I was frightened; nothing more! The swoon was nothing. You know, Betty, I am subject to such fits.

BETTY: But I had never seen you in so deep a swoon before.

SARA: Do not tell me so, please! I must have caused you a great deal of trouble, my good girl.

BETTY: Marwood herself seemed moved by your danger. In spite of all I could do she would not leave the room, until you had opened your eyes a little and I could give you the medicine.

SARA:	After all I must consider it fortunate that I swooned. For who knows what more I should have had to hear from her! She certainly can hardly have followed me into my room without a purpose! You cannot imagine how terrified I was. The dreadful dream I had last night recurred to me suddenly, and I fled, like an insane woman who does not know why and whither she flies. But Mellefont does not come. Ah!
BETTY:	What a sigh, Miss! What convulsions!
SARA:	God! What sensation was this –
BETTY:	What was that?
SARA:	Nothing, Betty! A pain! Not one pain, a thousand burning pains in one! But do not be uneasy; it is over now!

SCENE TWO

Norton, Sara, Betty.

NORTON:	Mellefont will be here in a moment.
SARA:	That is well, Norton! But where did you find him?
NORTON:	A stranger had enticed him beyond the town gate, where he said a gentleman waited for him, to speak with him about matters of the greatest importance. After taking him from place to place for a long time, the swindler slunk away from him. It will be bad for him if he lets himself be caught. Mellefont is furious.
SARA:	Did you tell him what has happened?
NORTON:	All.
SARA:	But in such a way! –
NORTON:	I could not think about the way. Enough! He knows what anxiety his imprudence has again caused you.
SARA:	Not so, Norton; I have caused it myself.
NORTON:	Why may Mellefont never be in the wrong? Come in, sir; love has already excused you.

SCENE THREE

Mellefont, Norton, Sara, Betty.

MELLEFONT: Ah, Sara! If this love of yours were not –

SARA: Then I should certainly be the unhappier of the two. If nothing more vexatious has happened to you in your absence than to me. I am happy.

MELLEFONT: I have not deserved to be so kindly received.

SARA: Let my weakness be my excuse, that I do not receive you more tenderly. If only for your sake, I would that I was well again.

MELLEFONT: Ha! Marwood! This treachery too! The scoundrel who led me with a mysterious air from one street to another can assuredly have been a messenger of her only! See, dearest Sara, she employed this artifice to get me away from you. A clumsy artifice certainly, but just from its very clumsiness, I was far from taking it for one. She shall have her reward for this treachery. Quick, Norton, go to her lodging; do not lose sight of her, and detain her until I come!

SARA: What for, Mellefont? I intercede for Marwood.

MELLEFONT: Go!

Exit Norton.

SCENE FOUR

Sara, Mellefont, Betty.

SARA: Pray let the wearied enemy who has ventured the last fruitless assault retire in peace! Without Marwood I should be ignorant of much –

MELLEFONT: Much? What is the "much"?

SARA: What you would not have told me, Mellefont! You start! Well, I will forget it again, since you do not wish me to know it.

MELLEFONT: I hope that you will not believe any ill of me which has no better foundation than the jealousy of an angry slanderer.

SARA: More of this another time! But why do you not tell me first of all about the danger in which your precious life was placed? I, Mellefont, I should have been the one who had sharpened the sword, with which Marwood had stabbed you.

MELLEFONT: The danger was not so great. Marwood was driven by blind passion, and I was cool, so her attack could not but fail. I only wish that she may not have been more successful with another attack – upon Sara's good opinion of her Mellefont! I must almost fear it. No, dearest Sara, do not conceal from me any longer what you have learned from her.

SARA: Well! If I had still had the least doubt of your love, Mellefont, Marwood in her anger would have removed it. She surely must feel that through me she has lost that which is of the greatest value to her; for an uncertain loss would have let her act more cautiously.

MELLEFONT: I shall soon learn to set some store by her bloodthirsty jealousy, her impetuous insolence, her treacherous cunning! But Sara! You wish to evade my question and not to reveal to me –

SARA: I will; and what I said was indeed a step towards it. That Mellefont loves me, then, is undeniably certain. If only I had not discovered that his love lacked a certain confidence, which would be as flattering to me as his love itself. In short, dearest Mellefont – Why does a sudden anxiety make it so difficult for me to speak? – Well, I suppose I shall have to tell it without seeking for the most prudent form in which to say it. Marwood mentioned a pledge of love; and the talkative Norton – forgive him, pray – told me a name – a name, Mellefont, which must rouse in you another tenderness than that which you feel for me.

MELLEFONT: Is it possible? Has the shameless woman confessed her own disgrace? Alas, Sara, have pity on my confusion! Since you already know all, why do you wish to hear it again from my lips? She shall never come into your sight – the unhappy child, who has no other fault than that of having such a mother.

SARA: You love her, then, in spite of all?

MELLEFONT: Too much, Sara, too much for me to deny it.

SARA: Ah, Mellefont! How I too love you, for this very love's sake! You would have offended me deeply, if you had denied the sympathy of your blood for any scruples on my account. You have hurt me already in that you have threatened me never to let her come into my sight. No, Mellefont! That you will never forsake Arabella must be one of the promises which you vow to me in the presence of the Almighty! In the hands of her mother she is in danger of becoming unworthy of her father. Use your authority over both, and let me take the place of Marwood. Do not refuse me the happiness of bringing up for myself a friend who owes her life to you – a Mellefont of my own sex. Happy days, when my father, when you, when Arabella will vie in your calls on my filial respect, my confiding love, my watchful friendship. Happy days! But, alas! They are still far distant in the future. And perhaps even the future knows nothing of them, perhaps they exist only in my own desire for happiness! Sensations, Mellefont, sensations which I never before experienced, turn my eyes to another prospect. A dark prospect, with awful shadows! What sensations are these?

Puts her hand before her face.

MELLEFONT: What sudden change from exultation to terror! Hasten, Betty! Bring help! What ails you, generous Sara! Divine soul! Why does this jealous hand (*Moving it away.*) hide these sweet looks from me? Ah, they are looks which unwillingly betray cruel pain. And yet this hand is jealous to hide these looks from me. Shall I not share your pain with you? Unhappy man, that I can only share it – that I may not feel it alone! Hasten, Betty!

BETTY: Whither shall I hasten?

MELLEFONT: You see, and yet ask? For help!

SARA: Stay. It passes over. I will not frighten you again, Mellefont.

MELLEFONT: What has happened to her, Betty? These are not merely
the results of a swoon.

SCENE FIVE

Norton, Mellefont, Sara, Betty.

MELLEFONT: You are back again already, Norton? That is well! You
will be of more use here.

NORTON: Marwood is gone –

MELLEFONT: And my curses follow her! She is gone? Whither? May
misfortune and death, and, were it possible, a whole
hell lie in her path! May Heaven thunder a consuming
fire upon her, may the earth burst open under her, and
swallow the greatest of female monsters!

NORTON: As soon as she returned to her lodgings, she threw
herself into her carriage, together with Arabella and her
maid, and hurried away, at full gallop. This sealed note
was left behind for you.

MELLEFONT: *(Taking the note.)* It is addressed to me. Shall I read it,
Sara?

SARA: When you are calmer, Mellefont.

MELLEFONT: Calmer? Can I be calmer, before I have revenged
myself on her, and before I know that you are out of
danger, dearest Sara?

SARA: Let me not hear of revenge! Revenge is not ours. – But
you open the letter. Alas, Mellefont! Why are we less
prone to certain virtues with a healthy body, which
feels its strength, than with a sick and wearied one?
How hard are gentleness and moderation to you, and
how unnatural to me appears the impatient heat of
passion! Keep the contents for yourself alone.

MELLEFONT: What spirit is it that seems to compel me to disobey
you? I opened it against my will, and against my will I
must read it!

SARA: *(Whilst Mellefont reads to himself.)* How cunningly man
can disunite his nature, and make of his passions

another being than himself, on whom he can lay the
blame for that which in cold blood he disapproves. –
The water, Betty! I fear another shock, and shall need
it. Do you see what effect the unlucky note has on
him? Mellefont! You lose your senses, Mellefont! God!
he is stunned! Here, Betty. Hand him the water! He
needs it more than I.

MELLEFONT: *(Pushing Betty back.)* Back, unhappy girl! Your
medicines are poison!

SARA: What do you say? Recover yourself! You do not
recognise her.

BETTY: I am Betty – take it!

MELLEFONT: Wish rather, unhappy girl, that you were not she!
Quick! Fly, before in default of the guiltier one you
become the guilty victim of my rage.

SARA: What words! Mellefont, dearest Mellefont –

MELLEFONT: The last "dearest Mellefont" from these divine lips,
and then no more for ever! At your feet, Sara. . . .
(Throwing himself down.) But why at your feet?
(Springing up again.) Disclose it? I disclose it to you?
Yes! I will tell you, that you will hate me, that you
must hate me? You shall not hear the contents, no,
not from me. But you will hear them. You will. . . .
Why do you all stand here, stock still, doing nothing?
Run, Norton, bring all the doctors! Seek help, Betty!
Let your help be as effective as your error! No, stop
here! I will go myself –

SARA: Whither, Mellefont? Help for what? Of what error do
you speak?

MELLEFONT: Divine help, Sara! Or inhuman revenge! You are lost,
dearest Sara! I too am lost! Would the world were lost
with us!

SCENE SIX

Sara, Norton, Betty.

SARA: He is gone! I am lost? What does he mean? Do you

understand him, Norton? I am ill, very ill; but suppose the worst, that I must die, am I therefore lost? And why does he blame you, poor Betty? You wring your hands? Do not grieve: you cannot have offended him; he will bethink himself. Had he only done as I wished, and not read the note! He could have known that it must contain the last poisoned words from Marwood.

BETTY: What terrible suspicion! No, it cannot be. I do not believe it!

NORTON: *(Who has gone towards the back of the stage.)* Your father's old servant, Miss.

SARA: Let him come in, Norton.

SCENE SEVEN

Waitwell, Sara, Betty, Norton.

SARA: I suppose you are anxious for my answer, dear Waitwell. It is ready except a few lines. But why so alarmed? They must have told you that I am ill.

WAITWELL: And more still.

SARA: Dangerously ill? I conclude so from Mellefont's passionate anxiety more than from my own feelings. Suppose, Waitwell, you should have to go with an unfinished letter from your unhappy Sara to her still more unhappy father! Let us hope for the best! Will you wait until tomorrow? Perhaps I shall find a few good moments to finish off the letter to your satisfaction. At present, I cannot do so. This hand hangs as if dead by my benumbed side. If the whole body dies away as easily as these limbs . . . you are an old man, Waitwell, and cannot be far away from the last scene. Believe me, if that which I feel is the approach of death, then the approach of death is not so bitter. Ah! Do not mind this sigh! Wholly without unpleasant sensation it cannot be. Man could not be void of feeling; he must not be impatient. But, Betty, why are you so inconsolable?

BETTY: Permit me, Miss, permit me to leave you.

SARA: Go; I well know it is not everyone who can bear to be with the dying. Waitwell shall remain with me! And you, Norton, will do me a favour, if you go and look for your master. I long for his presence.

BETTY: *(Going)* Alas, Norton, I took the medicine from Marwood's hands!

SCENE EIGHT

Waitwell, Sara.

SARA: Waitwell, if you will do me the kindness to remain with me, you must not let me see such a melancholy face. You are mute! Speak, I pray! And if I may ask it, speak of my father! Repeat all the comforting words which you said to me a few hours ago. Repeat them to me, and tell me too, that the Eternal Heavenly Father cannot be less merciful. I can die with that assurance, can I not? Had this befallen me before your arrival, how would I have fared? I should have despaired, Waitwell. To leave this world burdened with the hatred of him, who belies his nature when he is forced to hate – what a thought! Tell him that I died with the feelings of the deepest remorse, gratitude and love. Tell him – alas, that I shall not tell him myself – how full my heart is of all the benefits I owe to him. My life was the smallest amongst them. Would that I could yield up at his feet the ebbing portion yet remaining!

WAITWELL: Do you really wish to see him, Miss?

SARA: At length you speak – to doubt my deepest, my last desire!

WAITWELL: Where shall I find the words which I have so long been vainly seeking? A sudden joy is as dangerous as a sudden terror. I fear only that the effect of his unexpected appearance might be too violent for so tender a heart!

SARA: What do you mean? The unexpected appearance of whom?

WAITWELL: Of the wished-for one! Compose yourself!

SCENE NINE

Sir William Sampson, Sara, Waitwell.

SIR WILLIAM: You stay too long, Waitwell! I must see her!

SARA: Whose voice –

SIR WILLIAM: Oh, my daughter!

SARA: Oh, my father! Help me to rise, Waitwell, help me to
                  rise that I may throw myself at his feet. *(She endeavours
                  to rise and falls back again into the arm-chair.)* Is it he,
                  or is it an apparition sent from Heaven like the angel
                  who came to strengthen the Strong One? Bless me,
                  whoever thou art, whether a messenger from the
                  Highest in my father's form or my father himself!

SIR WILLIAM: God bless thee, my daughter! Keep quiet. *(She tries
                  again to throw herself at his feet.)* Another time, when
                  you have regained your strength, I shall not be
                  displeased to see you clasp my faltering knees.

SARA: Now, my father, or never! Soon I shall be no more! I
                  shall be only too happy if I still have a few moments to
                  reveal my heart to you. But not moments – whole days
                  – another life, would be necessary to tell all that a
                  guilty, chastened and repentant daughter can say to an
                  injured but generous and loving father. My offence,
                  and your forgiveness –

SIR WILLIAM: Do not reproach yourself for your weakness, nor give
                  me credit for that which is only my duty. When you
                  remind me of my pardon, you remind me also of my
                  hesitation in granting it. Why did I not forgive you at
                  once? Why did I reduce you to the necessity of flying
                  from me? And this very day, when I had already
                  forgiven you, what was it that forced me to wait first for
                  an answer from you? I could already have enjoyed a
                  whole day with you if I had hastened at once to your
                  arms. Some latent spleen must still have lain in the
                  innermost recesses of my disappointed heart, that I
                  wished first to be assured of the continuance of your
                  love before I gave you mine again. Ought a father to
                  act so selfishly? Ought we only to love those who love
                  us? Chide me, dearest Sara! Chide me! I thought more

of my own joy in you than of you yourself. And if I
were now to lose this joy? But who, then, says that I
must lose it? You will live; you will still live long.
Banish all these black thoughts! Mellefont magnifies
the danger. He put the whole house in an uproar, and
hurried away himself to fetch the doctors, whom he
probably will not find in this miserable place. I saw his
passionate anxiety, his hopeless sorrow, without being
seen by him. Now I know that he loves you sincerely;
now I do not grudge him you any longer. I will wait
here for him and lay your hand in his. What I would
otherwise have done only by compulsion. I now do
willingly, since I see how dear you are to him. Is it true
that it was Marwood herself who caused you this
terror? I could understand this much from your Betty's
lamentations, but nothing more. But why do I inquire
into the causes of your illness, when I ought only to be
thinking how to remedy it. I see you growing fainter
every moment. I see it and stand helplessly here. What
shall I do, Waitwell? Whither shall I run? What shall I
give her? My fortune? My life? Speak!

SARA: Dearest father! All help would be in vain! The dearest
help, purchased with your life, would be of no avail.

SCENE TEN

Mellefont, Sara, Sir William, Waitwell.

MELLEFONT: Do I dare to set my foot again in this room? Is she still
alive?

SARA: Step nearer, Mellefont!

MELLEFONT: Am I to see your face again? No, Sara; I return
without consolation, without help. Despair alone brings
me back. But whom do I see? You, Sir? Unhappy
father! You have come to a dreadful scene! Why did
you not come sooner? You are too late to save your
daughter! But, be comforted! You shall not have come
too late to see yourself revenged.

SIR WILLIAM: Do not remember in this moment, Mellefont, that we have ever been at enmity! We are so no more, and we shall never be so again. Only keep my daughter for me, and you shall keep a wife for yourself.

MELLEFONT: Make me a god, and then repeat your prayer! I have brought so many misfortunes to you already, Sara, that I need not hesitate to announce the last one. You must die! And do you know by whose hand you die?

SARA: I do not wish to know it – that I can suspect it is already too much –

MELLEFONT: You must know it, for who could be assured that you did not suspect wrongly? Marwood writes thus: *(He reads.)* "When you read this letter, Mellefont, your infidelity will already be punished in its cause. I had made myself known to her and she had swooned with terror. Betty did her utmost to restore her to consciousness. I saw her taking out a soothing-powder, and the happy idea occurred to me of exchanging it for a poisonous one. I feigned to be moved, and anxious to help her, and prepared the draught myself. I saw it given to her, and went away triumphant. Revenge and rage have made me a murderess; but I will not be like a common murderess who does not venture to boast of her deed. I am on my way to Dover; you can pursue me, and let my own handwriting bear witness against me. If I reach the harbour unpursued I will leave Arabella behind unhurt. Till then I shall look upon her as a hostage. Marwood." Now you know all, Sara! Here, Sir, preserve this paper! You must bring the murderess to punishment, and for this it is indispensable. – How motionless he stands!

SARA: Give me this paper, Mellefont! I will convince myself with my own eyes. *(He hands it to her and she looks at it for a moment.)* Shall I still have sufficient strength? *(Tears it.)*

MELLEFONT: What are you doing, Sara!

SARA: Marwood will not escape her fate; but neither you nor my father shall be her accusers. I die, and forgive the hand through which God chastens me. Alas, my father, what gloomy grief has taken hold of you? I love you still, Mellefont, and if loving you is a crime, how guilty shall I enter yonder world! Would I might hope, dearest father, that you would receive a son in place of a daughter! And with him you will have a daughter, too, if you will acknowledge Arabella as such. You must fetch her back, Mellefont; her mother may escape. Since my father loves me, why should I not be allowed to deal with this love as with a legacy? I bequeath this fatherly love to you and Arabella. Speak now and then to her of a friend from whose example she may learn to be on her guard against love. A last blessing, my father! – Who would venture to judge the ways of the Highest? – Console your master, Waitwell! But you too stand there in grief and despair, you who lose in me neither a lover nor a daughter?

SIR WILLIAM: We ought to be giving you courage, and your dying eyes are giving it to us. No more, my earthly daughter – half angel already; of what avail can the blessing of a mourning father be to a spirit upon whom all the blessings of heaven flow? Leave me a ray of the light which raises you so far above everything human. Or pray to God, who hears no prayer so surely as that of a pious and departing soul – pray to Him that this day may be the last of life also!

SARA: God must let the virtue which has been tested remain long in this world as an example; only the weak virtue which would perhaps succumb to too many temptations is quickly raised above the dangerous confines of the earth. For whom do these tears flow, my father? They fall like fiery drops upon my heart; and yet – yet they are less terrible to me than mute despair. Conquer it, Mellefont! – My eyes grow dim. – That sigh was the last! But where is Betty? – Now I understand the wringing of her hands. – Poor girl! – Let no one reproach her with carelessness, it is excused by a heart without falsehood, and without suspicion of it. – The moment is come! Mellefont – my father –

Dies.

MELLEFONT: She dies! Ah, let me kiss this cold hand once more. *(Throwing himself at her feet.)* No! I will not venture to touch her. The old saying that the body of the slain bleeds at the touch of the murderer, frightens me. And

who is her murderer? Am I not he, more than
Marwood? *(Rises)* She is dead now, Sir; she does not
hear us any more. Curse me now. Vent your grief in
well-deserved curses. May none of them miss their
mark, and may the most terrible be fulfilled twofold!
Why do you remain silent? She is dead! She is
certainly dead. Now, again, I am nothing but
Mellefont! I am no more the lover of a tender
daughter, whom you would have reason to spare in
him. What is that? I do not want your compassionate
looks! This is your daughter! I am her seducer. Bethink
yourself, Sir! In what way can I rouse your anger? This
budding beauty, who was yours alone, became my
prey! For my sake her innocent virtue was abandoned!
For my sake she tore herself from the arms of a
beloved father! For my sake she had to die! You make
me impatient with your forbearance, Sir! Let me see
that you are a father!

SIR WILLIAM: I am a father, Mellefont, and am too much a father not
to respect the last wish of my daughter. Let me
embrace you, my son, for whom I could not have paid
a higher price!

MELLEFONT: Not so, Sir! This angel enjoined more than human
nature is capable of! You cannot be my father. Behold,
Sir *(Drawing the dagger from his bosom.)*, this is the
dagger which Marwood drew upon me today. To my
misfortune, I disarmed her. Had I fallen a guilty victim
of her jealousy, Sara would still be living. You would
have your daughter still, and have her without
Mellefont. It is not for me to undo what is done – but
to punish myself for it is still in my power!

He stabs himself and sinks down at Sara's side.

SIR WILLIAM: Hold him, Waitwell! What new blow upon my stricken
head! Oh, would that my own might make the third
dying heart here.

MELLEFONT: *(Dying)* I feel it. I have not struck false. If now you will
call me your son and press my hand as such, I shall die
in peace. *(Sir William embraces him.)* You have heard of
an Arabella, for whom Sara pleaded; I should also
plead for her; but she is Marwood's child as well as

mine. What strange feeling seizes me? Mercy – O
Creator, mercy!

SIR WILLIAM: If the prayers of others are now of any avail, Waitwell,
let us help him to pray for this mercy! He dies! Alas!
He was more to pity than to blame.

SCENE ELEVEN

Norton, The others.

NORTON: Doctors, Sir! –

SIR WILLIAM: If they can work miracles, they may come in! Let me
no longer remain at this deadly spectacle! One grave
shall enclose both. Come and make immediate
preparations, and then let us think of Arabella. Be she
who she may, she is a legacy of my daughter!

Exeunt.

THE END

MINNA VON BARNHELM

CHARACTERS

MAJOR VON TELLHEIM   (Discharged)

MINNA VON BARNHELM

COUNT VON BRUCHSALL   (Her uncle)

FRANZISKA   (Her maid)

JUST   (Servant to the major)

PAUL WERNER   (Former sergeant-major to the major)

LANDLORD

A LADY IN MOURNING

A DISPATCH-RIDER

RICCAUT DE LA MARLINIÈRE

The action takes place alternately in the hall of an inn and an adjoining room.

ACT ONE

SCENE ONE

Just.

JUST: *(Sitting in a corner and talking in his sleep.)* You're a louse, Landlord! You, you . . . Quick, mate! . . . Hit him! *(Swings a punch and wakes.)* Hullo, at it again? I can't have a snooze without dreaming I'm at his throat. If I'd landed just half of those punches! . . . What's this? It's morning. I'll have to go and hunt up my poor master. I tell you, if it was up to me, he'd never set foot in this damned house again. Now just where's he spent the night, I wonder.

SCENE TWO

LANDLORD: Good morning, Herr Just, good morning! My, you're up early, or should I say you're still up late?

JUST: Say what you like.

LANDLORD: I only wished you 'Good morning', and I would have thought that Herr Just could have thanked me for that.

JUST: Thank you.

LANDLORD: A man gets peevish when he doesn't get his proper rest. I'll bet the Major didn't come home, and you've been waiting up for him here.

JUST: What a brilliant piece of deduction!

LANDLORD: Guesswork, just guesswork.

JUST: *(Turns and makes to leave.)* Your servant!

LANDLORD: No, no, Herr Just!

JUST: Fine then, I'm not your servant!

LANDLORD: Hey, Herr Just! I do hope you're not still angry from yesterday? What man will keep his anger overnight?

JUST: I will; and for all the nights to come.

LANDLORD: Is that Christian?

JUST: It's as Christian as pushing an honest man out of your
            house, throwing him out onto the street because he
            can't pay up at once.

LANDLORD: Shame; who could be so godless?

JUST: A Christian landlord. . . . And my master! What a
            man! What an officer!

LANDLORD: I pushed *him* out of my house? Threw him out onto
            the street? I have much too much respect for officers,
            and much too much pity for them, when they're
            discharged ever to do that! Out of necessity I had to
            move him into another room. . . . Think no more of it,
            Herr Just. *(Calls off.)* Hey, there! . . . I'd like to make
            it up to you another way. *(Enter Boy.)* Bring a glass;
            Herr Just will take a little glass with me, the good
            stuff!

JUST: Don't put yourself out, Landlord. The drink would
            poison me, the . . . no, I mustn't swear on an empty
            stomach!

LANDLORD: *(To the Boy who enters with a bottle of liqueur and a
            glass.)* Give it here, and get out! Now, Herr Just,
            something quite exceptional; strong, delightful and
            wholesome. *(Fills a glass and hands it to him.)* That will
            set your stomach right after a sleepless night!

JUST: I shouldn't really! But why should I let my health
            suffer on account of your insolence? *(Takes it and
            drinks.)*

LANDLORD: Your health, Herr Just!

JUST: *(Giving the glass back.)* Not bad! But you're still a rat,
            Landlord!

LANDLORD: Come on, come on! Quick, have another. It's no good
            standing on one leg.

JUST: I must say it's good, very good! . . . Make it yourself?

LANDLORD: God forbid! It's genuine Danziger! Look, the twin
            salmon mark.

JUST: Look, Landlord; if I was a hypocrite, that's the stuff that would win me over. But I'm not, so I've got to say it: You're a rat.

LANDLORD: In the whole of my life, no-one's ever called me that. . . . Have another, Herr Just; all good things come in threes!

JUST: If you like! *(Drinks)* Good stuff, really good stuff! . . . But the truth is good stuff too . . . And you're still a rat, Landlord!

LANDLORD: Would I let you talk to me like this if I was?

JUST: Oh yes, rats aren't renowned for their guts.

LANDLORD: Just one more, Herr Just? A chair needs four legs!

JUST: No, enough is enough! And what's the point, Landlord? I'd stick by what I'm saying to the last drop in the bottle. What a shame, Landlord, to have such good Danziger and such bad manners! . . . A man like my master, who's lodged with you for years, and who's given you a good few Talers, and who, all his life, has never owed anyone a penny, just because he hasn't paid up on the nail for a couple of months, and hasn't been spending as much . . . in his absence, you go and clear out his room!

LANDLORD: But it was because I had to have the room. And I knew that the Major would have been happy to have moved out himself, if we'd had the time to wait for his return. Should I have turned away such an illustrious visitor instead, then? Should I have thrown such good business into the jaws of another landlord? And I don't believe for a moment that she would have found a room anywhere else. All the inns are jammed full at the moment. Should I have let such a young, beautiful and charming lady stay on the street? Your master's too much of a gentleman for that! And what's he lost, then? Haven't I moved him into another room instead?

JUST: Behind the dovecot, with a view of next-door's wall . . .

LANDLORD: The view was really nice until those blasted neighbours started building. But apart from that, the room's quite elegant, it's papered . . .

JUST: It *was* papered!

LANDLORD: Come on, one wall still is. And what's wrong with your
               little room next door? It's got a fireplace. I'll admit it
               does smoke a bit in the winter . . .

JUST: But it looks very pretty in the summer. . . . I'm
               beginning to think, Sir, that you are trying to make
               fools of us up there?

LANDLORD: Now, now, Herr Just, Herr Just . . .

JUST: I'd advise you not to get me all steamed up, or . . .

LANDLORD: That's not me, that's the Danziger! . . .

JUST: An officer like my master! Or have you got the idea
               that a discharged officer is no longer an officer capable
               of breaking your neck for you? You landlords were all
               over us during the war. All the officers were worthy
               men then, and all the soldiers were stout-hearted,
               gallant fellows. It doesn't take much peace to make you
               insolent again, does it?

LANDLORD: What are you getting all worked up for now, Herr Just?

JUST: Because I want to get worked up . . .

SCENE THREE

Von Tellheim, Landlord, Just.

TELLHEIM: *(Entering)* Just!

JUST: *(Thinking the Landlord's addressing him.)* Oh, it's Just
               now, is it?

TELLHEIM: Just!

JUST: I was under the impression I was Herr Just to you.

LANDLORD: Shush! Herr Just . . . look around; your Master . . .

TELLHEIM: Just, I believe you're squabbling? What were my
               orders?

LANDLORD: Oh, your Honour! Squabbling? God forbid! Would

your most humble servant make so bold as to squabble
with someone who had the honour to be your
servant?

JUST: Just let me give him one up his grovelling
            backside . . .

LANDLORD: It's true, Herr Just was speaking up for his master, and
            got a bit heated. But he was right to; I esteem him all
            the more for it, I love him for it . . .

JUST: Let me knock his teeth out for him!

LANDLORD: It's just a shame that he got himself heated for nothing.
            For I am sure that your Honour will not hold it against
            me that I . . . was obliged . . . by necessity . . .

TELLHEIM: Say no more, Sir! I am obliged to you. You have
            cleared out my room in my absence; you must be paid;
            I must seek accommodation elsewhere. But of course!

LANDLORD: Elsewhere? You want to move out, your Honour? Oh
            misery! Oh ruination! No, never! The lady will just
            have to move out again. The Major will not, cannot
            give up his rooms; the rooms are his; she must get out;
            there's nothing I can do for her . . . I'll go now, your
            Honour . . .

TELLHEIM: My friend, don't add insult to injury! The lady must
            remain in possession of the rooms . . .

LANDLORD: But your Honour will think that it was out of mistrust,
            out of anxiety about my payment. . . . As if I didn't
            know that your Honour could pay me at any moment
            he chose to. . . . The sealed pouch . . . with five
            hundred Louis d'Or written on it . . . which your
            Honour put in the writing desk . . . is in safe keeping
            . . .

TELLHEIM: I hope so; like the rest of my things. Just will take
            charge of them, when he has paid your bill . . .

LANDLORD: I don't mind telling you I got a shock when I found
            that pouch . . . I've always taken your Honour to be a
            tidy, provident sort of a person, who'd never spend all
            he'd got. . . . But still. . . . If I'd thought there was
            ready money in the writing desk . . .

TELLHEIM:	You would have behaved a little more politely towards me. I understand you. . . . Now go away, Sir; leave me; I must speak to my servant . . .
LANDLORD:	But, your Honour . . .
TELLHEIM:	Come Just, this gentleman will not permit me to give you your instructions in his house . . .
LANDLORD:	I'm going, I'm going, your Honour! . . . My whole house is at your disposal.

SCENE FOUR

Von Tellheim, Just.

JUST:	*(Stamps his foot and spits after the Landlord.)* Ugh!
TELLHEIM:	What's the matter?
JUST:	I'm choking with rage.
TELLHEIM:	That sounds like apoplexy.
JUST:	And you . . . I no longer recognise you, Sir. May I drop dead at your feet if you're not acting as guardian angel to this malicious, merciless rat. I'd risk the gallows, the sword and the wheel to . . . throttle him with these hands, to tear him apart with these teeth . . .
TELLHEIM:	Animal!
JUST:	Better an animal than a man like that!
TELLHEIM:	So, what is it you want?
JUST:	I want you to be aware of how deeply you've been wronged.
TELLHEIM:	Then what?
JUST:	Then revenge yourself . . . no, the louse is too low for you . . .
TELLHEIM:	Or perhaps give you the task of revenging me? That was my intention from the start. He shall not see my face again, and shall receive his payment from your hands. I am sure you could throw him a handful of gold with a contemptuous look . . .

JUST: What? That's a fine revenge! . . .

TELLHEIM: But one we will still have to postpone. I haven't a
               penny in cash, and don't know where to raise any.

JUST: No cash? So what's that pouch with the five hundred
               Louis d'Or that the Landlord found in the desk, then?

TELLHEIM: That's money which was given me to look after.

JUST: Not the hundred Pistoles your old Sergeant-Major
               brought you four or five weeks ago?

TELLHEIM: The same; from Paul Werner. Why not?

JUST: You haven't used them yet? Sir, you can do what you
               like with those, I'll answer for them.

TELLHEIM: Really?

JUST: Werner heard from me how they were taking their time
               over your claim on the Army Treasury. He heard . . .

TELLHEIM: That I was sure to be reduced to beggary, if I was not
               so already . . . I am much obliged to you, Just . . . and
               this news induced Werner to share what little he has
               with me. . . . Well, I'm glad I've found this out. . . .
               Listen, Just, make me out your account at once. We'll
               part company . . .

JUST: What? What?

TELLHEIM: Not another word; someone's coming.

SCENE FIVE

A Lady in mourning, Von Tellheim, Just.

LADY: Oh, excuse me, Sir . . .

TELLHEIM: Who are you looking for, Madam? . . .

LADY: The very gentleman I have the honour to address. You
               do not remember me? I am the widow of your former
               Captain of Horse . . .

TELLHEIM: Heavens, Madam, what a change in you!

LADY: I have just come from the sickbed to which the pain of
               losing my husband confined me. But I have no wish to

bore you. The point is that I am travelling to the
country, where a kind-hearted, but equally
impoverished friend has offered me a refuge for now
. . .

TELLHEIM: *(To Just.)* Go, leave us alone . . .

SCENE SIX

The Lady, Von Tellheim.

TELLHEIM: Speak freely, Madam! You need not feel ashamed of
your misfortune in my presence. Can I offer you any
assistance?

LADY: My dear Major . . .

TELLHEIM: I commiserate with you, Madam! How can I be of
assistance to you? You know your husband was my
friend; I mean my friend; and I have always been
sparing with that title.

LADY: Who knows better than I how worthy you were of his
friendship, and how worthy he was of yours? You
would have been his last thought, your name the last
sound on his dying lips, had not nature reserved that
sad privilege for his unfortunate son and his
unfortunate wife . . .

TELLHEIM: Stop, Madam! I would gladly weep with you, but I
have no tears today. Spare me! You have found me at a
time, when I might easily be enticed into grumbling
against providence. . . . Oh, my honest Marloff!
Quickly, Madam, tell me what I can do. If I am in a
position to help you, if I can . . .

LADY: I must not set off before I have carried out his last
request. Shortly before the end he remembered that he
would die in debt to you, and he implored me to pay
off this debt with the first money I had. I have sold his
equipment, and I have come to redeem his note.

TELLHEIM: What, Madam? Is that why you have come?

LADY: Yes. Allow me to count you out the money.

TELLHEIM: No, Madam! Marloff in debt to me? That seems

unlikely. Let me see. *(Takes out and looks through his pocket book.)* I can't find anything.

LADY: You must have mislaid his note; anyway, the note doesn't matter . . . Allow me to . . .

TELLHEIM: No Madam! I am not in the habit of mislaying such things. If I no longer have it, that proves that I never had it, or that it was redeemed, and has already been returned.

LADY: Major!

TELLHEIM: It's certain, Madam, Marloff owed me nothing. I really cannot recall that he ever owed me anything. What's more, Madam, he has rather left me in his debt. I have never been able to do enough to recompense a man who shared with me six years of good times and bad, honour and danger. I will not forget that he leaves a son. He shall be my son, as soon as I am in a position to act as a father to him. The difficulties in which I find myself at the moment . . .

LADY: How generous you are! But don't think too poorly of me either. Take the money, Major, to set my mind at rest.

TELLHEIM: What could set your mind at rest better than the assurance that the money does not belong to me? Or would you have me rob the innocent orphan of my friend? Rob, Madam, for that is what it would be, nothing less. It belongs to him, put it by for him! . . .

LADY: I understand; please forgive me for not yet knowing how to receive kindnesses. How is it that you too know that a mother will do more for her son than for her own life? I'll go . . .

TELLHEIM: Yes, go, Madam! Bon voyage! I will not ask you to send me news of you. It may arrive at a time when I cannot make use of it. But, there is something else, Madam. I almost forgot the most important thing. Marloff still has an outstanding claim with the treasury of our old regiment. His claim is as good as mine. If mine is met, then his will be too. I shall take care of that . . .

LADY: Oh, Sir! . . . But I'll say nothing. To prepare such future kindnesses is in God's eye to have given them already. May you receive His reward, and my tears of gratitude.

Exit.

SCENE SEVEN

Von Tellheim.

TELLHEIM: Poor, brave woman! I must not forget to destroy the note. *(Takes papers from his pocket-book and tears them up.)* What guarantee do I have that my own necessity might not one day betray me into using them?

SCENE EIGHT

Just, Von Tellheim.

TELLHEIM: Are you there?

JUST: *(Wiping his eyes.)* Yes!

TELLHEIM: Have you been crying?

JUST: I was in the kitchen writing out my bill, and the kitchen's full of smoke.

TELLHEIM: Give it here.

JUST: Have pity on me, Sir. I know very well that people have none for you, but . . .

TELLHEIM: What do you mean?

JUST: I'd have thought I had more chance of dying than getting dismissed.

TELLHEIM: I can't use you any more. I must learn to manage without servants. *(Opens the bill and reads.)* 'What the Major owes me: Three and a half month's wages at six Talers a month; makes twenty-one Talers. Since the first of this month, sundry expenses: one Taler, seven Groschen, nine Pfennigs . . . sum total: Twenty-two Talers, seven Groschen, nine Pfennigs'. Good, and it's

only fair that I should pay you for the rest of the
current month.

JUST: The other side, Major . . .

TELLHEIM: There's more? *(Reads)* 'What I owe the Major: Paid to
             the regimental surgeon on my behalf: Twenty-five
             Talers. For nursing care during my convalescence, paid
             for me thirty-nine Talers. To my father, whose house
             was raided and burned down, advanced, at my request:
             fifty Talers, not including the two captured horses he
             sent him. Sum total: One hundred and fourteen Talers.
             Deduct therefrom the aforesaid twenty-two Talers,
             seven Groschen, nine Pfennigs; that leaves me owing
             the Major ninety-one Talers, sixteen Groschen and
             three Pfennigs' . . . You're mad!

JUST: I'm sure I've cost you a lot more. But it would have
             been a waste of ink to add any more. I can't repay you,
             and even if you take all my livery away, which I
             haven't paid for . . . Oh, why didn't you let me peg
             out in the hospital?

TELLHEIM: What do you take me for? You owe me nothing, and I
             will recommend you to one of my acquaintances, with
             whom you will be better off than with me.

JUST: I don't owe you anything, and you still want to get rid
             of me?

TELLHEIM: Because I don't want to owe you anything.

JUST: Is that all? . . . As certain as it is that I owe you
             money, and that you could never owe me anything, it's
             just as certain that you mustn't send me away. . . . Do
             what you like, Major, I'm going to stay with you. I've
             got to stay with you . . .

TELLHEIM: And your obstinacy, your insolence, your rough, wild
             behaviour with everyone who has no hold over you,
             your gloating over others' misfortunes, your
             vindictiveness . . .

JUST: Paint me as black as you like; I won't think any the
             worse of me than I do of my dog. Last winter I was
             walking along the canal at dusk when I heard
             something whimpering. I climbed down and reached

out to the noise, thinking I was going to rescue a child, but, instead, I pulled a poodle out of the water. 'Fine', I thought. But the poodle followed me. Well now, I'm no lover of poodles. I chased him off; no good. I whipped him away; no good. I wouldn't let him into my room at night, so he stayed outside on the doorstep. When he came too near me, I shoved him away with my foot; he howled, looked at me and wagged his tail. He's never had a crumb to eat from my hand, and I'm still the only person he'll obey, and the only one who can touch him. He runs in front of me and does tricks for me, without my asking him to. He's ugly for a poodle, but he's a wonderful dog. If he keeps on like this, I suppose, in the end, I shall have to stop hating poodles.

TELLHEIM: *(Aside)* As I him! No, nobody can be that inhuman!
             . . . Just, we'll stay together.

JUST: Yes Sir! You manage without a servant? You're forgetting your wounds, and that you only have the use of one arm. Why, you can't even dress by yourself. I'm indispensable to you; and I am . . . without boasting, Major . . . I am a servant, who . . . if the worst came to the worst . . . knows how to beg and steal for his master.

TELLHEIM: Just, we'll have to part company.

JUST: Yes Sir!

SCENE NINE

A Servant, Von Tellheim, Just.

SERVANT: Oi! Mate!

JUST: What's up?

SERVANT: Can you help me find the officer who had this room here until yesterday? *(Points in the direction from which he entered.)*

JUST: That's easy. What have you brought for him?

SERVANT: What you always bring when you bring nothing: compliments. My lady hears that he has been driven

out on her account. My lady knows her manners, and
so I am here to beg his pardon.

JUST: Well, beg his pardon. There he is.

SERVANT: Who is he? What's he called?

TELLHEIM: My friend, I have heard your message. It is an
               unnecessary politeness on your mistress's part, which I
               recognise as I ought. Give her my compliments. . . .
               What is her Ladyship's name?

SERVANT: Her name? I just call her: 'Madam'.

TELLHEIM: And her family name?

SERVANT: I haven't heard that yet, and it's not my place to ask. I
               work it so I usually have a new master or mistress
               every six weeks. The Devil take their names!

JUST: Bravo, Mate!

SERVANT: I joined this one just a few days ago in Dresden. I
               think she's looking for her fiancé . . .

TELLHEIM: Enough, my friend. I was interested in her Ladyship's
               name, not her secrets. Away with you!

SERVANT: I say, Mate, he's not my kind of master!

SCENE TEN

Von Tellheim, Just.

TELLHEIM: Just, see to it that we quit this house! I find the
               politeness of this unknown lady more painful than the
               rudeness of the landlord. Here, take this ring. It is the
               last thing of value I have left, and which I would never
               have foreseen my using in this fashion! Pawn it! Raise
               eighty Friedrichs d'Or on it; the landlord's bill can't
               amount to more than thirty. Pay him, and remove my
               things . . . Yes, where to? . . . Oh, wherever you like.
               The cheaper the inn the better. You'll find me at the
               coffee house next door. I'll go now. Make a good job of
               it . . .

JUST: Don't worry, Major!

TELLHEIM:	*(Coming back.)* Above all, make sure you don't forget my Pistoles; the pouch is hanging behind the bed.
JUST:	I won't forget anything.
TELLHEIM:	*(Coming back again.)* One more thing: be sure to bring your poodle along with you, do you hear, Just?

SCENE ELEVEN

Just.

JUST:	The poodle won't get left behind, I'll let him take care of that himself. . . . Hm! So the Master still had this expensive ring, did he? And had it in his pocket instead of on his finger? Well, Landlord, we're not as skint as we look. I'll pledge you with him, and no-one else, my pretty little ring! I bet he'll be furious when he knows we won't be spending all of you in his house! . . .

SCENE TWELVE

Paul Werner, Just.

JUST:	Well, look who's here! Werner! Hullo! Welcome to town.
WERNER:	That damned village! I just couldn't get used to it again. Happy days, boys; I've got some more money! Where's the Major?
JUST:	You must have passed him. He's just gone down the stairs.
WERNER:	I came up the back way. Now, how is he? I would have been with you a week ago, but . . .
JUST:	Well, what kept you?
WERNER:	. . . Just. . . . Have you heard of Prince Heraclius?
JUST:	Heraclius? I don't think so.
WERNER:	You don't know the great hero of the East?
JUST:	I know about three wise men from the East who wander about after a star at Christmas . . .

WERNER: I don't believe you read the papers any more than the
           Bible. . . . You don't know about Prince Heraclius, the
           brave man who has taken Persia, and very soon is going
           to burst open the Ottoman Porte? Thank God there's
           still a war somewhere in the world! I've been waiting
           around long enough in the hope that it'll start again
           here. But there they all sit, saving their skins. No! I
           was a soldier before, and I must be a soldier again! In
           short . . . *(Looking around him to see if anyone is
           listening.)* between you and me, Just, I'm going off to
           Persia to fight a couple of campaigns under His Royal
           Highness Prince Heraclius against the Turks.

JUST: You?

WERNER: Me, as true as I'm standing here. Our forefathers were
           always marching against the Turks, and so should we,
           if we want to be honest fellows and good Christians. I
           grant you a campaign against the Turks won't be half
           as much fun as one against the French; but for that
           very reason it must be more rewarding, both in this
           world and the one to come. Your Turks all have sabres
           set with diamonds . . .

JUST: I wouldn't go out of my way to get my head split by a
           sabre like that. You're not going to be mad enough to
           leave that lovely farm of yours?

WERNER: No, I'm taking it with me! . . . You know what? I've
           sold the farm . . .

JUST: Sold it?

WERNER: Shush! . . . Here's a hundred Ducats I got from the
           sale yesterday. I was bringing them to the Major . . .

JUST: And what's he meant to do with them?

WERNER: Do with them? Spend them! Let him drink, let him
           gamble, let him. . . . It's up to him. The man needs
           money, and it's a bad show that they're making such
           difficulties about his! But I know just what I'd do, if I
           was in his position! I'd say: 'The Devil take the lot of
           you here; I'm off to Persia with Paul Werner'. Damn
           it! Prince Heraclius must surely have heard of Major
           Tellheim, even if he doesn't know his old sergeant-
           major. That business at the Katzenberg . . .

JUST: Shall I tell you this time?

WERNER: You tell me? . . . I can see that your heart has got the
            better of your head. Well, I'm not going to cast my
            pearls before swine. . . . Here, take the hundred
            Ducats; give them to the Major. Tell him to put them
            by for me as well. I must go to the market. I've sent
            two bushels of rye for sale there. He can have whatever
            they fetch as well . . .

JUST: Werner, you mean well, but we don't want your
            money. Keep your Ducats, and you can have your
            hundred Pistoles back too, untouched, whenever you
            like.

WERNER: I see. Has the Major still got some money then?

JUST: No.

WERNER: Has he borrowed some?

JUST: No.

WERNER: Then what's he living on?

JUST: We've been living on credit, and when people won't
            give us any more credit, and throw us out, we pawn
            what we have left, and go on from there. . . . Listen,
            Paul, we must play a trick on the landlord here.

WERNER: Has he been annoying the Major? . . . I'm your man!

JUST: What about waylaying him at night, when he's coming
            out of the tavern, and giving him a good hiding?

WERNER: At night? . . . Waylay him? . . . Two against one? . . .
            That's no good.

JUST: What about burning his house down around him?

WERNER: Pillaging and burning? . . . You can tell you were a
            baggage lad, and no soldier. . . . No!

JUST: What about making a whore of his daughter? Mind
            you, she's bloody ugly . . .

WERNER: That'll have happened long since! Anyway, you'd need
            no help for that. But what's up? What is it?

JUST: Come on, you'll be surprised!

WERNER: All hell's been let loose, then.

JUST: Right; come on!

WERNER: All the better! And then off to Persia, to Persia.

END OF ACT ONE

ACT TWO

SCENE ONE

The Lady's room.

Minna, Franziska,

MINNA: *(In a negligée, looking at her watch.)* Franziska, we seem
           to have risen very early. The time will hang on our
           hands.

FRANZISKA: It's hopeless trying to sleep in these confounded big
           cities. What with the coaches, the watchmen, the
           drums, the cats, the corporals . . . there's no end to
           their clattering, screaming, drumming, miaowing, and
           swearing; it seems the last thing you're meant to do at
           night is rest. . . . a cup of tea, Madam?

MINNA: I don't like tea.

FRANZISKA: I'll get them to make some of our chocolate.

MINNA: For yourself, then, not for me.

FRANZISKA: For me? I'd just as soon talk to myself as drink by
           myself. . . . Yes, the time's going to hang on our hands
           alright. . . . We'll have to dress soon, and sort out
           which gown to wear to make the first assault.

MINNA: Why talk of assaults when I have come here merely to
           demand unconditional surrender?

FRANZISKA: And this officer we've driven out, and to whom we've
           sent our apologies; he can't have very good manners or
           he would have begged for permission to call on us by
           now.

MINNA: Not every officer is a Tellheim. To tell you the truth, it
           was only to gain an opportunity of making enquiries
           about him that I sent our apologies. . . . Franziska, my
           heart tells me that I shall be lucky in my quest, and
           that I shall find him.

FRANZISKA: Your heart, Madam? People shouldn't trust their hearts
           too far. They are all too willing to say what you want to

hear. If our mouths were as ready to flatter as our hearts, it would have become the fashion long ago to keep our mouths under lock and key.

MINNA: Ha, ha! One's mouth under lock and key? The fashion seems a good one to me.

FRANZISKA: Better to hide pretty teeth than to open your mouth and bare your heart as well!

MINNA: What? Are you so reserved?

FRANZISKA: No, Madam; but I'd like to be. People don't talk much about the virtues they have, but all the more about those they haven't got.

MINNA: You know, Franziska, you've just made a very perceptive remark.

FRANZISKA: Made? Can you make something that just occurs to you?

MINNA: And do you know why I find this remark so perceptive? It's because it applies so well to my Tellheim.

FRANZISKA: What is there for you that doesn't apply to him?

MINNA: Friend and foe alike say that he is the bravest man in the world. But who has ever heard him speak of bravery? He is the soul of integrity, but integrity and generosity are words that are never on his lips.

FRANZISKA: What virtues does he speak of, then?

MINNA: None, because he has them all.

FRANZISKA: I just wanted to hear you say that.

MINNA: Wait, Franziska; I remember now. He often speaks of economy. Between ourselves, Franziska, I believe the man's a spendthrift.

FRANZISKA: Another thing, Madam. I have often heard him talk of his faithfulness and constancy towards you. What if he was fickle?

MINNA: You wretched creature! . . . But do you mean that seriously, Franziska?

FRANZISKA: Well, how long is it since he last wrote to you?

MINNA: Ah! Since the peace he has written to me only once.

FRANCISKA: Now you're sighing against the peace! That's
              wonderful! Peace ought only to right the wrongs caused
              by war, but, instead, it's ruining the good the war
              brought about. Peace ought to be more considerate! . . .
              and how long have we been at peace now? The time will
              drag if it brings so little news! What's the point of the
              post working again, if nobody's writing, because
              nobody's got anything to write about?

MINNA: 'Now there's peace', he wrote to me, 'and I am
              approaching the fulfilment of my wishes'. But the fact
              that he has written only once, one single letter . . .

FRANZISKA: That he is compelling us ourselves to hurry towards
              this 'fulfilment of wishes'. Just let's find him and make
              him pay for that! . . . What if, in the meantime, the
              man's 'fulfilled his wishes', and we find out here . . .

MINNA: *(Anxious and excited.)* That he is dead?

FRANZISKA: To you, Madam, in the arms of another . . .

MINNA: Torturer! Just wait, Franziska, he'll make you pay for
              that! . . . But keep talking or we shall fall asleep
              again. . . . His regiment was disbanded after the peace.
              Who knows what a tangle of accounts and enquiries he
              must be facing? Who knows to what other regiment,
              in what far-flung province he has been transferred?
              Who knows in what circumstances. . . . Someone's
              knocking.

FRANZISKA: Come in.

SCENE TWO

Landlord, Minna, Franziska.

LANDLORD: *(Sticking his head round the door.)* Might I, your
              Ladyship?

FRANZISKA: Our dear Landlord? . . . Come right in.

LANDLORD: *(A pen behind his ear, a sheet of paper and an inkstand in
              his hand.)* I have come, your Ladyship, to wish you a

humble 'Good Morning' . . . *(To Franziska.)* and you too, my pretty child . . .

FRANZISKA: What a courteous man!

MINNA: We thank you.

FRANZISKA: And wish you too a 'Good Morning'.

LANDLORD: Might I presume to enquire how your Ladyship rested the first night under my poor roof?

FRANZISKA: It's not the roof that's poor, but the beds that could do with improvement.

LANDLORD: What's that I hear? Not rested well? Perhaps the excessive exhaustion of the journey . . .

MINNA: Perhaps so.

LANDLORD: I'm sure of it, I'm sure of it! . . . Meanwhile if there is anything you lack for your Ladyship's comfort, you need only to ask.

FRANZISKA: Very well, Landlord! We're not shy, you know. Anyway, an inn is the last place where you can afford to be shy. We'll tell you what we want.

LANDLORD: And now I must also . . . *(Taking the pen from behind his ear.)*

FRANZISKA: Well?

LANDLORD: No doubt your Ladyship is already acquainted with the wise precautions taken by our police.

MINNA: Not in the least, Landlord.

LANDLORD: We landlords are directed not to accommodate any stranger, of whatever rank or station, for twenty-four hours without submitting, in writing, in the proper quarter, his name, his home, his character, his business here, the probable duration of his stay, and so on.

MINNA: Quite right.

LANDLORD: Perhaps your Ladyship will be so kind as to . . .

MINNA: With pleasure. . . . My name is . . .

LANDLORD: Just one moment, please! . . . *(He writes.)* 'Date: the twenty-second of August anni currentis; arrived here at

the King of Spain' . . . now your names, your
Ladyship?

MINNA: Das Fräulein von Barnhelm.

LANDLORD: *(Writing)*: 'von Barnhelm'. . . . Coming . . . from
where, your Ladyship?

MINNA: From my estates in Saxony.

LANDLORD: *(Writing):* 'Estates in Saxony' . . . Saxony! Ay, ay, from
Saxony, your Ladyship? Saxony?

MINNA: Well? Why not? It is surely not a sin in these parts to
be from Saxony?

LANDLORD: A sin? God forbid! That would be quite a new sin! . . .
From Saxony then? Well, well, from Saxony! Dear old
Saxony! . . . but if I remember rightly, your Ladyship,
Saxony is a large place, and has several . . . what shall I
say? . . . districts, provinces. . . . Our police are very
particular, your Ladyship.

MINNA: I understand. From my estates in Thuringia, then.

LANDLORD: From Thuringia! Yes, that's better, your Ladyship,
more precise . . . *(Writes and reads.)* 'Das Fräulein von
Barnhelm, coming from her estates in Thuringia, with a
waiting woman and two servants . . .'

FRANZISKA: A waiting woman? That's supposed to be me, is it?

LANDLORD: Yes, my pretty child.

FRANZISKA: Now then, Landlord, instead of waiting woman, put
down lady's maid. I have heard your police are very
particular. There might be a misunderstanding and
some trouble when my banns are called. For I *am* still a
maid, and I'm called Franziska, surname Willig. I come
from Thuringia too. My father was a miller on one of
her Ladyship's estates. It's called Klein-Rammsdorf.
My brother has the mill now. I came to court when I
was very young, and was brought up with her
Ladyship. We are of an age; twenty-one next
Candlemas. I have learned everything her Ladyship
has. I shall be delighted for the police to know
everything about me.

LANDLORD: Very well, my pretty one, I'll remember that in case of further enquiries. And now, your Ladyship, your business here?

MINNA: My business?

LANDLORD: Does it concern His Majesty?

MINNA: Oh no!

LANDLORD: Or the High Court of Justice?

MINNA: Nor that.

LANDLORD: Or . . .

MINNA: No, no. I am here on a purely private matter.

LANDLORD: Of course, your Ladyship, but how would you describe this private matter?

MINNA: I would describe it . . . Franziska, I believe we are being interrogated.

FRANZISKA: Surely the police won't want to learn a Lady's secrets?

LANDLORD: Certainly, my pretty one. The police want to know everything, and secrets most of all.

FRANZISKA: Well, your Ladyship, what's to be done? . . . Now listen here, Landlord, . . . as long as this stays between us and the police!

MINNA: What is the little fool going to tell him?

FRANZISKA: We have come to kidnap one of the King's officers.

LANDLORD: What? What? My child! My child!

FRANZISKA: Or to be kidnapped by the officer. It's all the same.

MINNA: Franziska, are you mad? . . . She's pulling your leg, Landlord.

LANDLORD: I hope not! She can joke as much as she likes with your humble servant, but with the esteemed police . . .

MINNA: Do you know what, Landlord? . . . I am not sure how to handle this. I would think you could leave all this registration business until my uncle arrives. I told you yesterday the reason why he did not arrive at the same time as us. He had an accident two leagues from here, and was insistent that this unfortunate occurrence should not delay me another night. I had to proceed. He will be here no later than twenty-four hours after me.

LANDLORD: Very well, your Ladyship, we will await his arrival, then.

MINNA: He will be better able to answer your questions. He will know to whom, and how far he may declare himself; what of his affairs he may reveal, and what keep secret.

LANDLORD: All the better. You certainly can't expect a young girl *(Looking significantly at Franziska.)* to treat a serious matter in a serious way with serious people.

MINNA: And his rooms are in readiness, are they, Landlord?

LANDLORD: Completely, your Ladyship, completely; all except one . . .

FRANZISKA: Which you have to throw some honest man out of first, perhaps?

LANDLORD: The lady's maids in Saxony are full of sympathy, your Ladyship.

MINNA: But it was not right of you, Landlord. You should have declined to take us in.

LANDLORD: But why, your Ladyship, why?

MINNA: I hear that the officer whom we have ousted . . .

LANDLORD: He's only a discharged officer, your Ladyship . . .

MINNA: So!

LANDLORD: Who's on his way out . . .

MINNA: So much the worse! He may be a very deserving man.

LANDLORD: I'm telling you he's been discharged.

MINNA: The King cannot know all deserving men.

LANDLORD: Oh, certainly he does, he knows them all.

MINNA: Well, he cannot reward them all.

LANDLORD: Those who have shown they deserve a reward will have got one. But during the war these gentlemen have been

living as if the war would last for ever; there were no
such words as 'yours' or 'mine'. Now all the inns and
hotels are full of them; and a landlord has to keep a
close eye on them. I did all right with this one. Even if
he had no ready money left, he had stuff that was as
good as cash, and I would have quite happily let him
stay for two or three months more. Still, it's best to be
on the safe side. . . . By the way, your Ladyship, you
must know something about jewellery?

MINNA: Not particularly.

LANDLORD: Your Ladyship should do, no? . . . I must show you a
ring, an expensive ring. Well, I can see that your
Ladyship has a very pretty ring on her finger too, and
the more I look at it, the more surprised I am at how
much like mine it looks. . . . Just have a look, have a
look! (*Takes the ring out of its case and hands it to the
ladies.*) What fire; the centre brilliant alone weighs
over five carats.

MINNA: (*Looking at him.*) Where am I? What am I seeing? This
ring . . .

LANDLORD: Is worth a good fifteen hundred Talers.

MINNA: Franziska! . . . Look here!

LANDLORD: I didn't hesitate to lend him eighty Pistoles on it.

MINNA: Don't you recognise it, Franziska?

FRANZISKA: The very one! Landlord, where did you get this ring?

LANDLORD: What, my child. Surely you've not got a claim on it?

FRANZISKA: We have no claim on this ring?! The inside of the case
must bear the Lady's monogram. . . . Show him,
Madam.

MINNA: It's the one, it is! . . . How did you come by this ring,
Landlord?

LANDLORD: Me? In the most honest way in the world. . . . Your
Ladyship, your Ladyship, you're not going to ruin me,
surely? How should I know where the ring comes
from? During the war a lot of things changed hands,
with or without the knowledge of the owners. War is
war. There's more than one ring come over the border

from Saxony. . . . Give me it back, your Ladyship, give me it back.

FRANZISKA: Tell us first who you got it from.

LANDLORD: I wouldn't have thought he went in for that sort of thing. He's a good man otherwise . . .

MINNA: He's the best man under the sun, if you had it from its owner. . . . Quickly, bring the man to me! It's him, or at least someone who knows him.

LANDLORD: Who then? Who, your Ladyship?

FRANZISKA: Aren't you listening? Our Major.

LANDLORD: Major? That's right, it was a major who had this room before you, and it was him I got it from.

MINNA: Major von Tellheim?

LANDLORD: Von Tellheim, yes! Do you know him?

MINNA: Do I know him! Is he here! Is Tellheim here? He lodged in this room? He, he pawned this ring with you? How has he got into difficulties? Where is he? Is he in debt to you? . . . Franziska, the strong box! Open it! *(Franziska puts it on the table and opens it.)* What does he owe you? Who else is he in debt to? Bring me all his creditors. Here is money. Here are bills. Everything is his!

LANDLORD: What's that you're saying?

MINNA: Where is he? Where is he?

LANDLORD: He was still here an hour ago.

MINNA: You loathsome man! How could you be so unkind, so hard, so cruel to him?

LANDLORD: Forgive me, your Ladyship . . .

MINNA: Quickly, produce him here for me.

LANDLORD: His servant might still be here. Would your Ladyship like me to go and find him?

MINNA: Would I? Hurry, run. For this service alone I will overlook the shameful way in which you have treated him . . .

FRANZISKA: Shift, Landlord, quick, off with you!

        Pushes him out.

SCENE THREE

Minna, Franziska.

MINNA: I've found him again, Franziska! Do you see, I've found him! I'm beside myself with joy! Come on, rejoice with me, dear Franziska. But you're right, why should you? No, you should, you must rejoice with me. Come, my dear, I want to give you something so that you can rejoice with me. Tell me, Franziska, what shall I give you? Which of my things would suit you best? What would you like? Take whatever you want, only rejoice. I can see that you will not accept anything. Wait! *(Reaches into a satchel.)* There, my dear Franziska, *(Giving her money.)* buy something you'd like. Ask for more, if that isn't enough. Only rejoice with me. It's a sorry business being happy by oneself. Take it . . .

FRANZISKA: It would be stealing, Madam. You are drunk, drunk with happiness . . .

MINNA: I'm quarrelsome drunk, my girl. Take it or . . . *(Pressing money into her hand.)* . . . Don't you dare thank me! . . . Wait. I'm glad I thought of this. *(Reaches into the satchel for money.)* Put this aside, my dear Franziska, for the first poor wounded soldier to appeal to us for alms.

SCENE FOUR

Landlord, Minna, Franziska.

MINNA: Well? Is he coming?

LANDLORD: That offensive, ill-bred lout!

MINNA: Who?

LANDLORD: His servant. He refuses to take the message.

FRANZISKA: Just you bring the rascal here . . . I'm well acquainted
            with all the Major's servants. Which one's this, then?

MINNA: Bring him here quickly. When he sees us, he'll go fast
            enough.

            Exit Landlord.

SCENE FIVE

MINNA: I can't wait for the moment. . . . But, Franziska, you're
            still so cold. Will you still not rejoice with me?

FRANZISKA: I would with all my heart, if only . . .

MINNA: Only what?

FRANZISKA: We have found the man again, but *how* will we find
            him? From what we've heard, he must be in a bad way.
            He must be in trouble. That's what upsets me.

MINNA: That upsets you? . . . Let me embrace you, my darling
            playmate! I will never forget that! . . . I am merely in
            love, but you are truly good . . .

SCENE SIX

Landlord, Just, Minna, Franziska.

LANDLORD: I've had enough trouble getting him here.

FRANZISKA: A strange face! I don't know him.

MINNA: My friend, are you with Major von Tellheim?

JUST: Yes.

MINNA: Where is your Master?

JUST: Not here.

MINNA: But you know where to find him?

JUST: Yes.

MINNA: Will you be kind enough to fetch him here at once?

JUST:	No.
MINNA:	You would be doing me a favour . . .
JUST:	Ah!
MINNA:	And your Master a service . . .
JUST:	Perhaps not . . .
MINNA:	Why should you think that?
JUST:	Well, you're the strange lady who sent him her compliments this morning, aren't you?
MINNA:	Yes.
JUST:	So there you are.
MINNA:	Does your Master know my name?
JUST:	No, but he has about as much time for over-civil ladies as he has for over-rude landlords.
LANDLORD:	I suppose that's meant for me.
JUST:	Yes.
LANDLORD:	Still, don't make her Ladyship pay for that. Go and fetch him here at once.
MINNA:	Franziska, give him something . . .
FRANZISKA:	*(Trying to push money into Just's hand.)* We don't expect your services for nothing.
JUST:	Nor I your money for nothing.
FRANZISKA:	The one in return for the other.
JUST:	I can't do it. My Master has ordered me to move out of here. That's what I'm doing now, and I would ask you not to keep me from my work any longer. When I've finished, I daresay I'll tell him he can come here. He's next door in the coffee house. And if he's got nothing better to do, I daresay he might come. *(Makes to leave.)*
FRANZISKA:	Just a minute. . . . Her Ladyship is the Major's . . . sister . . .
MINNA:	Yes, yes, his sister.

JUST: I know better than that. The Major hasn't got a sister.
                In the last six months he's twice sent me to his family in
                Courland. . . . Mind you, there's sisters and sisters . . .

FRANZISKA: You impudent . . .

JUST: I need to be, some of the errands I have to run.

                    Exit.

FRANZISKA: What a lout!

LANDLORD: I told you so. But let him be! I know where his master
                is now. I'll go and fetch him myself straight away. . . .
                Only might I humbly ask your Ladyship if you would
                offer the Major my humble apologies, that I, against
                my will, had the misfortune to . . . a man of his
                distinction . . .

MINNA: Just go at once, Landlord. I will put everything to
                rights.

                    Exit Landlord.

                Franziska, run after him: he's not to mention my name!

                    Exit Franziska.

SCENE SEVEN

Minna, later Franziska.

MINNA: I've found him again! . . . Am I alone? . . . I must not
                squander my time alone. *(Folds her hands.)* Nor am I
                alone! A single, grateful thought to heaven is the best
                of all prayers! . . . I've found him! I've found him!
                (Spreads her arms.) I am happy! And joyful! What could
                please the Creator more than to see a joyful creature?
                . . . *(Enter Franziska.)* Are you returned, Franziska?
                . . . Do you pity him? I don't pity him. Misfortune can
                also be a blessing. Perhaps heaven has taken all he has
                to return it all in me!

FRANZISKA: He might be here at any moment. . . . You are still in
                your negligée, your Ladyship. What if you dressed
                quickly?

MINNA: No, leave me. In future he will see me oftener thus than fully dressed.

FRANZISKA: You know yourself so well, Madam.

MINNA: *(After a moment's thought.)* Truly, my child, you've hit the mark again.

FRANZISKA: Beauty is at its best unadorned.

MINNA: Must we be beautiful then? . . . Perhaps all that is necessary is that we feel beautiful. . . . No, if only I can seem beautiful to him! . . . Franziska, if all girls are as I feel now, then we are . . . strange creatures. . . . Tender and proud, virtuous and vain, sensual and pious. . . . You don't understand me. I can hardly understand myself. . . . Joy is intoxicating, turns one's head.

FRANZISKA: Compose yourself, Madam; I can hear someone coming.

MINNA: Compose myself? Should I receive him calmly, then?

SCENE EIGHT

Von Tellheim, Landlord, Minna, Franziska.

TELLHEIM: *(Entering, sees her and runs to her.)* Ah! My Minna! . . .

MINNA: *(Running towards him.)* Ah! My Tellheim! . . .

TELLHEIM: *(Suddenly stopping short and retreating.)* Forgive me, Madam . . . to find Fräulein von Barnhelm here . . .

MINNA: Cannot be so wholly unexpected to you? . . . *(Moves towards him, he moves away.)* May heaven forgive you that I am still Fräulein von Barnhelm! . . .

TELLHEIM: My dear Lady! . . . *(Stares at the Landlord and shrugs his shoulders.)*

MINNA: *(Notices the Landlord and motions to Franziska.)* My dear Sir . . .

TELLHEIM: If we are not both mistaken . . .

FRANZISKA: Hey, Landlord, who's this you've brought us, then? Come on, quick, let's go and find the right one.

LANDLORD: Isn't he the right one? I'm sure he is!

FRANZISKA: I'm sure he isn't! Come on, quick. I haven't said
             'Good morning' to your little daughter yet.

LANDLORD: Oh, highly honoured . . . *(Not moving from the spot.)*

FRANZISKA: *(Grabbing him.)* Come on we'll make out the menu. . . .
             Let's see what we're going to have . . .

LANDLORD: You're going to have: as a starter . . .

FRANZISKA: Shush, shush! If Madam knows now what she is going
             to have for lunch, she loses all her appetite. Come on,
             tell me on our own.

               Leads him out forcibly.

SCENE NINE

Von Tellheim, Minna.

MINNA: Well? Are we mistaken?

TELLHEIM: Would to heaven we were! . . . But there is only one,
             and you are she . . .

MINNA: How formal we are! When what we have to say is for
             everyone's ears.

TELLHEIM: You here? What do you seek here, Madam?

MINNA: I seek nothing more. *(Approaching him with open arms.)*
             All that I sought, I have found.

TELLHEIM: You sought a happy man, one worthy of your love, and
             have found . . . a poor wretch.

MINNA: Then you no longer love me? . . . And love another?

TELLHEIM: Madam, he never loved you, who could love another
             after you.

MINNA: You draw but one thorn from my soul. . . . If I have
             lost your heart, what does it matter whether
             indifference or more potent charms have brought me
             low? . . . You love me no more, and yet do not love
             another? Oh, you unfortunate man if you do not love at
             all! . . .

TELLHEIM: You are right, Madam. An unfortunate man must not love. He deserves his misfortune when he cannot maintain this victory over himself, when he allows those whom he loves to share in his ruin. . . . How hard is this victory! . . . Since reason and necessity demanded that I forget Minna von Barnhelm, how much effort it has cost me! I was just beginning to hope that this effort would not forever be in vain; and then you appear, Madam!

MINNA: Do I understand you aright? . . . One moment, Sir. Let us see where we stand, before we go any further astray. Will you answer me just one question?

TELLHEIM: Any, Madam.

MINNA: Will you answer without evasion and without subterfuge? With nothing but a plain 'Yes' or 'No'?

TELLHEIM: I will . . . if I can.

MINNA: You can. . . . Good. Notwithstanding the efforts to which you have gone to forget me . . . do you still love me, Tellheim?

TELLHEIM: Madam, this question . . . .

MINNA: You promised to answer with nothing but 'Yes' or 'No'.

TELLHEIM: And added: 'If I can'.

MINNA: You can. You must know what happens in your own heart. . . . Do you still love me, Tellheim? . . . Yes or No.

TELLHEIM: If my heart . . .

MINNA: Yes or No!

TELLHEIM: Well, yes!

MINNA: Yes?

TELLHEIM: Yes, yes! . . . Only . . .

MINNA: Wait! . . . You still love me; that's enough for me. . . . What a strange tone of voice I have caught from you: hostile and melancholy. . . . I must use my normal voice. . . . Well, my dear unfortunate, you love me still,

and still have your Minna, and you're unfortunate?
Listen what a conceited, silly creature your Minna was
. . . and is. She imagined . . . and still imagines that
she is all your fortune. Quickly, show her your
misfortune. She would like to see by how much she
outweighs it. . . . Well?

TELLHEIM: Madam, I am not accustomed to complain.

MINNA: Very good. Save boasting, I can think of nothing I
would find less pleasing in a soldier than complaining.
But there is a certain cool, casual way in which he may
speak of his bravery and his misfortune.

TELLHEIM: Which is, after all, only boasting and complaining.

MINNA: You're so obstinate. You should not have claimed to be
unfortunate at all. . . . You must either keep silent, or
tell me the whole story. . . . Reason and necessity
demanded that you forget me? . . . I am a great lover
of reason, and I have a great respect for necessity. . . .
But tell me now, how reasonable is this reason, and
how necessary this necessity?

TELLHEIM: Very well then, listen, Madam. You call me Tellheim;
that is my name. . . . But you think me that Tellheim
whom you knew in your homeland; the flourishing
man, full of expectations, full of ambition; master both
of his body and soul; before whom the doors of honour
and good fortune stood open; who, if not yet worthy of
your hand and heart, might daily hope to become
worthier of them. . . . I am as little that Tellheim as I
am my own father. Both are in the past. . . . I am the
discharged Tellheim, his honour wounded, a cripple,
and a beggar. . . . It was to the former you gave your
promise, Madam, will you keep it to the latter?

MINNA: That all sounds very tragic! . . . Still, Sir, until I find
the former again, I am so infatuated with these
Tellheims that I am prepared to make do with this one
for the moment. . . . Your hand, my dear beggar!

Takes his hand.

TELLHEIM: *(Covering his face with his hat and turning away from
her.)* This is too much! . . . Where am I? . . . Let me

go, Madam! . . . Your goodness is torturing me! . . .
Let me go.

MINNA: What is wrong? Where are you going?

TELLHEIM: Away from you.

MINNA: Away from me? *(Drawing his hand to her breast.)*
           Dreamer!

TELLHEIM: Despair will lay me dead at your feet.

MINNA: Away from me?

TELLHEIM: Away from you. . . . Never to see you again, never. . . .
           So resolved, so firmly resolved . . . not to commit a
           base act . . . nor to allow you to commit a rash one. . . .
           Let me go, Minna!

           Tears himself free and exit.

MINNA: *(Calling after him.)* You leave Minna? Tellheim!
           Tellheim!

                    END OF ACT TWO

ACT THREE

SCENE ONE

The Hall.

Just.

JUST: *(With a letter.)* Have I got to come into this damned house again? . . . A little letter from my Master to her Ladyship who claims to be his sister . . . I hope nothing comes of it . . . or there'll be no end to the comings and goings with letters . . . I'd like to be shot of it, but I don't fancy going in that room again. Those women-folk are as keen to ask questions as I am unwilling to answer them! . . . Ah, the door's opening. Perfect! the maid-serpent!

SCENE TWO

Franziska, Just.

FRANZISKA: *(Into the door through which she enters.)* Don't worry, I'll keep a look-out. . . . Well now! *(Seeing Just.)* I've had an idea already. But I'm not starting anything with this creature.

JUST: Your servant . . .

FRANZISKA: I can do without servants like you . . .

JUST: Now, now, forgive me my figure of speech! . . . I've brought a little letter from my Master to her Ladyship, Madam. . . . Sister. . . . Wasn't it? Sister.

FRANZISKA: Give it here! *(Grabs the letter from his hand.)*

JUST: My Master asks if you would be so kind as to deliver it. Then would you be so kind, my Master asks . . . now don't you go imagining, I don't know what! . . .

FRANZISKA: Well?

JUST: My Master knows his way about. He knows that the way to a lady lies through her maid. . . . I can just imagine! . . . Would the Maid, then, be so kind as to . . . my Master asks . . . let him know if he might have the pleasure of speaking to her for a few moments.

FRANZISKA: Me?

JUST: Forgive me, I thought you were still a maid! . . . Yes, you! . . . Just a few moments, but it must be alone, quite alone, in secret, just you and him. He has something very important to tell you.

FRANZISKA: Fine! I've got a good few things to tell him too. . . . Let him come; I'm at his service.

JUST: But when should he come? When's most convenient for you, my Maid? After dark, perhaps? . . .

FRANZISKA: What's that supposed to mean? . . . Your Master can come when he likes. . . . Now clear off!

JUST: With pleasure! *(Makes to go.)*

FRANZISKA: Listen. One more thing. . . . What's happened to the Major's other servants?

JUST: The others? They're here, there and everywhere.

FRANZISKA: Where's Wilhelm?

JUST: The valet? The Major let him go.

FRANZISKA: And Philipp, where's he?

JUST: The gamekeeper? Someone's taking care of him.

FRANZISKA: Because he doesn't hunt any more, I suppose. . . . But Martin? . . .

JUST: The coachman? He's ridden off.

FRANZISKA: And Fritz?

JUST: The messenger-boy? He's been promoted.

FRANZISKA: And where were you when the Major was in winter quarters with us in Thuringia? You weren't with him then, were you?

JUST: Oh yes; I was his groom, but I was in hospital.

FRANZISKA: Groom? And what are you now?

JUST: All in one: valet and gamekeeper, messenger-boy and
              groom.

FRANZISKA: Well I never! To dismiss all those able, smart fellows
              and to keep just the worst of the lot! I'd like to know
              what your Master sees in you!

JUST: Maybe he sees I'm reliable.

FRANZISKA: It's a poor look-out if you're no more than reliable. . . .
              Now Wilhelm was really something! . . . Your Master
              let him go, did he?

JUST: Yes, he let him go . . . because he didn't have a chance
              to stop him.

FRANZISKA: What?

JUST: Oh, Wilhelm should do well for himself on his travels.
              He's taken all the Major's clothes with him.

FRANZISKA: What? He's run off with them?

JUST: We can't say for certain, but he didn't follow on with
              them when we left Nuremberg.

FRANZISKA':   Oh, the villain!

JUST: He was an all-rounder. He could shave and curl and
              talk . . . and flirt . . . No?

FRANZISKA: Then I wouldn't have dismissed the gamekeeper, if I'd
              been the Major. Even if he couldn't use him as a
              gamekeeper, he was a fine fellow. . . . Who's looking
              after him, then?

JUST: The commandant of Spandau.

FRANZISKA: The prison? There can't be much game around the
              walls there.

JUST: That's not what he's doing there.

FRANZISKA: Then what is he doing?

JUST: Hard labour.

FRANZISKA: Hard labour?

JUST: It's only for three years. He hatched a little plot in my

	Master's company and tried to bring six men through the outposts.
FRANZISKA:	I'm amazed! The traitor!
JUST:	Oh, he was a fine fellow! A gamekeeper who knew all the paths and tracks through the woods and marshes for fifty miles around. And how he could shoot!
FRANZISKA:	It's lucky that the Major still has his honest coachman!
JUST:	Has he?
FRANZISKA:	I thought you said that Martin had ridden off? Surely he'll come back, won't he?
JUST:	Do you think so?
FRANZISKA:	Where's he ridden off to, then?
JUST:	It's ten weeks now since he rode off on the Master's last remaining horse . . . to the horse pond.
FRANZISKA:	And he's not come back yet? Oh, the gallows-bird!
JUST:	Perhaps the honest coachman has been swept away by the horse pond! . . . He was a splendid coachman! . . . He'd been driving in Vienna for ten years. The Master won't find another like him! When the horses were going flat out, all he had to say was 'Brr!' and suddenly they were standing stock still. He was an experienced vet as well!
FRANZISKA:	Now I'm afraid about the messenger-boy's promotion.
JUST:	No, no. That was regular enough. He's become a drummer with a garrison regiment.
FRANZISKA:	I thought as much!
JUST:	Fritz got involved with a disreputable woman, never came home at night, ran up debts everywhere in the Master's name, and played dirty tricks on everyone. In short, the Major could see that he wanted at all costs to go up in the world . . . *(Makes a gesture of hanging.)* . . . so he helped him on his way.
FRANZISKA:	Oh, the wretch!
JUST:	But he was a perfect messenger-boy, that's for sure. If the Master gave him fifty paces start, he couldn't catch

him, even with his fastest horse. But if Fritz gives the
gallows a thousand paces start, I'll bet my life it catches
up with him. . . . They were all good friends of yours,
weren't they, my Maid? Wilhelm and Philipp, Martin
and Fritz? . . . Well, now Just takes his leave!

Exit.

SCENE THREE

Franziska and later Landlord.

FRANZISKA: *(Looking after him, seriously.)* I deserved that. . . .
Thank you, Just. I did underrate honesty. I won't
forget my lesson! Oh, what an unfortunate man! *(Turns
and makes for Minna's room.)*

Enter Landlord.

LANDLORD: Wait a moment, my pretty child.

FRANZISKA: I've no time now, Landlord . . .

LANDLORD: Just a tiny moment! . . . Still no news from the Major?
That surely couldn't be his farewell? . . .

FRANZISKA: What couldn't?

LANDLORD: Has her Ladyship not told you? . . . After I left you,
my pretty child, in the kitchen, I came, quite by
chance, in here again . . .

FRANZISKA: Quite by chance, with the intention of eavesdropping.

LANDLORD: Oh, my child, how can you think such a thing of me?
There's nothing worse than an inquisitive landlord. . . .
I wasn't here long, before the door to her Ladyship's
room flew open. The Major dashed out, with her
Ladyship after him, both in a commotion, with such
looks, and in such a state . . . . I couldn't describe it.
She clasped him, he tore himself away, she clasped him
again. 'Tellheim!' . . . 'Let me go, Madam!' . . . 'Where
to?' . . . And so he pulled her with him to the top of
the stairs. I don't mind telling you, I was afraid he'd
drag her down with him. But he managed to break free.
Her Ladyship stayed standing on the top step staring
after him, calling after him, wringing her hands.

Suddenly she turned and ran to the window, then from the window to the stairs again, then down the stairs and to and fro in here. I was standing here, and she walked past me three times without seeing me. In the end she seemed to notice me, but, God bless us, I believe the Lady took me for you, my child. 'Franziska' she called, looking at me, 'am I happy now?' Then she looked up at the ceiling and said again: 'Am I happy now?' Then she wiped the tears from her eyes, and smiled, and asked me again: 'Franziska, am I happy now?' . . . I really didn't know where I was. Then she ran to the door, turned round to me again: 'Come on then, Franziska, whom do you pity now?'. . . And with that, she went in.

FRANZISKA: Oh, Landlord, you must have been dreaming.

LANDLORD: Dreaming? No, my pretty child, you don't dream details like that. . . . Yes, I'd give a good deal . . . *(Not wanting to pry.)* . . . but I'd give a good deal to have the key to all that.

FRANZISKA: The key? To our door? Landlord, we keep that on the inside. We take it in at night. We're timid.

LANDLORD: Not that key. No, I mean, my pretty child, the key, the explanation, as it were, the correct interpretation of what I saw.

FRANZISKA: Yes, indeed. . . . Well, goodbye, Landlord. Will lunch be ready soon?

LANDLORD: I mustn't forget what I particularly wanted to say.

FRANZISKA: Yes? But be quick about it . . .

LANDLORD: Her Ladyship still has my ring. I call it mine . . .

FRANZISKA: You won't lose it.

LANDLORD: That's not what I'm worried about. I just wanted to remind you. You see, I don't really want it back. I can work out why she knows the ring, and why it looks just like her own. It's in the best of safe keeping in her hands. I don't want it any more, so I'll just put the hundred Pistoles I gave for it on her Ladyship's account. That's alright, isn't it, my pretty child?

SCENE FOUR

Paul Werner, Landlord, Franziska.

WERNER: There he is, then!

FRANZISKA: A hundred Pistoles? I thought it was only eighty.

LANDLORD: That's true, ninety, only ninety. I'll see to that, my
               pretty child. I'll see to that.

FRANZISKA: Alright, Landlord.

WERNER: *(Approaches them from behind, and suddenly claps
               Franziska on the shoulder.)* Little Lady! Little Lady!

FRANZISKA: *(Terrified)* Hey!

WERNER: Don't be afraid, little Lady. I can see that you're
               pretty, and probably a stranger . . . and pretty strangers
               must be warned. . . . Little Lady, beware of this man!
               (Points to Landlord.)

LANDLORD: Oh, what an unexpected pleasure! Herr Paul Werner!
               You're welcome here, welcome. . . . Still the same jolly,
               joking, honest Werner! . . . You should beware of me,
               my pretty child? Ha, ha, ha!

WERNER: Just keep out of his way, that's all!

LANDLORD: Me! Me! . . . Am I that dangerous, then? . . . Just
               listen to him, my pretty child! How do you like his
               little joke?

WERNER: His sort always treat it as a joke, when you tell them
               the truth.

LANDLORD: The truth! Ha, ha, ha! . . . Better and better, my pretty
               child, no? What a joker! Me dangerous? . . . Me? . . .
               There might have been something in that twenty years
               ago. Yes, yes, my pretty one, I was dangerous then.
               There were a few who could have told you then. But
               now . . .

WERNER: No fool like an old fool!

LANDLORD: That's it exactly! When you get old, there's an end to
               any danger. . . . You won't fare any better, Herr
               Werner!

WERNER: Ye Gods, is there no end to it? . . . Little Lady, you'll
            credit me with enough sense not to be talking about
            that kind of danger. That devil may have left him, but
            seven others have taken its place! . . .

LANDLORD: Oh, listen, just listen to him! How he manages to twist
            everything you say! . . . Joke after joke, and always
            something new! Oh, you're a splendid man, Herr Paul
            Werner! . . . *(Whispers to Franziska.)* He's well off, and
            still single. Three miles from here he's got a freehold
            farm. He did well out of the war! . . . And rose to
            sergeant-major under our Herr Major. He's such a
            friend of the Major's, such a friend! He'd have himself
            shot for the Major!

WERNER: Yes! And he's such a friend of the Major, such a
            friend! . . . The sort the Major should have shot for
            himself.

LANDLORD: What? What? . . . No, Herr Werner, that's not a good
            joke. . . . Me no friend to the Major? No, I don't
            understand the joke.

WERNER: Just's told me a thing or two.

LANDLORD: Just? I might have guessed it was Just speaking
            through you. Just's a wicked, foul fellow. But here's a
            pretty child, who can tell you. She can say whether I'm
            a friend to the Herr Major or not? Whether I have
            been of service to him or not? And why shouldn't I be
            his friend? He's a worthy man, isn't he? It's true he's
            had the misfortune to be discharged, but what does
            that matter? The King can't know every worthy man,
            and if he did, he couldn't reward them all.

WERNER: God put those words into his mouth! . . . But Just . . .
            I grant you there's nothing special about Just, but he's
            no liar; and if it's true, what he said to me . . .

LANDLORD: I won't listen to anything from Just! As I said, let the
            pretty child here speak! *(Whispers to her.)* You know,
            my child, the ring! . . . Tell Herr Werner about it, and
            then he'll know me better. And just in case it looks as
            though she's saying what I want her to, I shan't even
            be present. I'll go. But you'll repeat my words, Herr
            Werner. . . . Just's a foul slanderer.

SCENE FIVE

Paul Werner, Franziska.

WERNER: Do you know the Major, then, Little Lady?

FRANZISKA: Major von Tellheim? Certainly, I know that fine man
            well.

WERNER: Isn't he a fine man? Do you admire him?

FRANZISKA: From the bottom of my heart.

WERNER: Really? That makes you as pretty again in my eyes. . . .
            But what are these services, then, that the Landlord
            claims to have performed for the Major?

FRANZISKA: I really can't imagine. Maybe he's trying to claim the
            credit for the good that has come by chance out of his
            knavery.

WERNER: So what Just told me was true? *(Turning towards the
            Landlord's exit.)* Lucky for you you've hopped it! . . .
            Has he really cleared his room out? . . . Playing a trick
            like that on such a gentleman, just because this
            numbskull imagines the gentleman has no more money!
            The Major no money?

FRANZISKA: Well, has the Major got money, then?

WERNER: He's made of money! He doesn't even know how much
            he's got. I owe him some myself, and I've come here to
            pay off the balance. Look, Little Lady, here in this bag
            (Draws a bag from his pocket.) are a hundred Louis
            d'Or; and in this bundle *(Draws a bundle from another
            pocket.)* a hundred Ducats, It's all his!

FRANZISKA: Really? But why, then, is the Major pawning things?
            He's pawned a ring that . . .

WERNER: Pawned? Don't you believe it. He probably wanted rid
            of the trifle.

FRANZISKA: It's not a trifle! It's a very expensive ring; and besides,
            he had it from the hands of a loved one.

WERNER: Well, that's it, then. From the hands of a loved one.
            Yes, yes, a thing like that ring will often remind you of
            something you'd rather forget. And: out of sight, out of
            mind.

FANZISKA: What?

WERNER: Funny things happen to a soldier in winter quarters.
              He's got nothing to do, so he takes a bit of trouble with
              his appearance, and in a little while he starts making
              acquaintances. Now he sees these friendships only
              lasting for the winter, but the good little soul with
              whom he has got acquainted is thinking in terms of a
              lifetime. Quick as a flash, a ring is slipped on his
              finger; he can't tell you how it got there. And often
              enough he'd be happy to lose the finger as well if he
              could only get shot of the ring.

FRANZISKA: Oh! But could that be the case with the Major?

WERNER: Certainly. Especially in Saxony. If he'd had ten fingers
              on each hand, he could have had rings on all twenty of
              them.

FRANZISKA: *(Aside)* This sounds very odd, and needs looking into
              . . . Sergeant-Major or should I say: 'Freeholder'? . . .

WERNER: If it's all the same with you, Little Lady, I'd rather be
              called Sergeant-Major.

FRANZISKA: Now, then, Sergeant-Major, I've got here a letter from
              the Major to my Lady. I'll just quickly take it in to
              her, and be back straight away. Will you be so good as
              to wait here that long? I'd really like to have a longer
              chat with you.

WERNER: Do you like chatting, Little Lady? Suits me. Run
              along. I like chatting too. I'll wait.

FRANZISKA: Do wait, please!

SCENE SIX

Paul Werner.

WERNER: Not a bad little lady that! . . . Still, I shouldn't have
              promised to wait for her. . . . Because the most
              important thing must be for me to find the Major. . . .
              He won't take my money, but goes pawning instead?
              . . . That's just like him. . . . I've got an idea. . . . When
              I was in town a fortnight ago, I paid a visit to Captain

Marloff's widow. The poor woman was on her sickbed, lamenting the fact that her husband had died still
owing the Major four hundred Talers, which she
couldn't see any way of repaying. I went to see her
again today. . . . I went to tell her that, when I get paid
the money for my farm, I could lend her five hundred
Talers. . . . I must put something by in case things
don't work out in Persia . . . but she's flown the nest.
And she certainly can't have paid the Major back. . . .
Yes, that's what I'll do. And the sooner the better. . . .
I hope the little lady won't take it amiss, but I can't
wait.

*Exit in thought, nearly walks into Tellheim, who
enters.*

SCENE SEVEN

TELLHEIM: You're preoccupied, Werner.

WERNER: Oh, there you are! I was just on my way to visit you in
             your new quarters, Major.

TELLHEIM: To fill my ears with cursing my old landlord, I
             suppose. Don't remind me.

WERNER: Yes, I would have done that too. But what I really had
             in mind was to thank you for being kind enough to
             look after the hundred Louis d'Or for me. Just has
             given them back. I would have been pleased if you
             could have kept them a while longer. But you've moved
             into quarters which aren't familiar to either of us. Who
             knows what might happen there. They might be stolen,
             and then you'd feel obliged to replace them, no two
             ways about it. I really can't expect you to do that.

TELLHEIM: *(Smiling)* Since when have you grown so prudent,
             Werner?

WERNER: I'm learning. Nowadays you can't be too careful with
             your money. . . . Speaking of which, I have something
             to deliver to you, Major, from Captain Marloff's
             widow. I've just come from her now. Her husband died
             owing you four hundred Talers, didn't he? Well, she is
             sending you one hundred Ducats on account. She'll

send you the rest next week. I could well be the reason why she can't send you the whole amount. You see, she owed me about eighty Talers, and as she thought I'd come to remind her . . . which was in fact the case . . . she paid me out of the bundle she'd already set aside for you. . . . But you can make do without the hundred Talers for a week better than I can without my few Groschen. . . . There, take it! *(Offers him a bundle of Ducats.)*

TELLHEIM: Werner!

WERNER: Well, what are you staring at me like that for? . . . Take it, Major! . . .

TELLHEIM: Werner!

WERNER: What's wrong? What's upset you?

TELLHEIM: *(Bitterly, striking his forehead and stamping.)* That . . . that the four hundred Talers aren't all there!

WERNER: Now, now, Major! Didn't you understand?

TELLHEIM: Oh, I understand perfectly! . . . Why is it that the best of people should be torturing me the worst of all today?

WERNER: What do you mean?

TELLHEIM: It's only half to do with you! . . . Go away, Werner! *(Pushing Werner's hand with the money away.)*

WERNER: I will, as soon as I'm rid of this.

TELLHEIM: Werner, what if I told you that Marloff's widow called on me herself earlier this morning?

WERNER: So?

TELLHEIM: And that she no longer owes me anything?

WERNER: Really?

TELLHEIM: That she paid me to the last penny. What would you say to that?

WERNER: *(After a moment's thought.)* I'd say that I'd lied to you, and that lying's a damn fool business, because you may get found out.

TELLHEIM:	And you're ashamed of yourself?
WERNER:	But what about the man who forced me into lying? How should he feel? Shouldn't he be ashamed of himself? Look, Major; if I was to say that your behaviour didn't annoy me, that would be another lie, and I don't want to lie any more . . .
TELLHEIM:	Don't be annoyed, Werner! I know your good heart and your love for me well! But I have no need of your money!
WERNER:	No need of it? You'd rather sell or pawn your things, and get yourself talked about?
TELLHEIM:	People may as well know that I've no money left. One should not seek to appear wealthier than one is.
WERNER:	But not poorer neither. . . . As long as your friends have got some, so have you.
TELLHEIM:	It would be unbecoming for me to be in your debt.
WERNER:	Unbecoming? . . . That day when we were hot from the sun and the enemy, and you'd lost your groom with the canteens, you came to me and said: 'Werner, have you anything to drink?' And I handed you my water bottle, didn't I, and you took a drink from it. . . . Was that becoming? . . . My God, if a drink of stale water at that moment wasn't worth more than all this trash! *(Reaches out with the bag of Louis d'Or, which he has taken out as well.)* Take them, my dear Major! Think of it as water. God made this too for us all.
TELLHEIM:	You're torturing me. Now listen, I will not be in your debt.
WERNER:	First it was unbecoming, now you will not. That's different. *(A little annoyed.)* You *will* not be in my debt! But what if you are already? Or are you not in debt to the man who parried the blow that would have split your skull, and, another time, struck off the arm that was about to fire a pistol at your breast? . . . What more could you owe this man? Or is it that my neck is worth less than my purse? . . . If you think that's noble, by God, you're wrong, it's idiotic!

TELLHEIM: Remember to whom you are speaking, Werner! We are alone, so I can say this. If a third person were here, it would be empty boasting. I am pleased to acknowledge that you have twice saved my life. But, my friend, had I had the opportunity, would I not have done the same for you? Well?

WERNER: No one doubts that you would, given the opportunity, Major. Haven't I seen you risk your life a hundred times for the commonest soldier in danger?

TELLEIM: Well?

WERNER: But . . .

TELLHEIM: Why will you not understand me? I am saying that it is not becoming for me to be in your debt; I will not be in your debt. That is to say, not in the circumstances I find myself in at present.

WERNER: So that's it! You want to wait until things look up. You'll borrow from me another time, when you don't need it, when you've got some, and perhaps I haven't.

TELLHEIM: One must not borrow, if one cannot see one's way to repaying the loan.

WERNER: Someone like you can't be short for ever.

TELLHEIM: You know what's what! . . . At the very least, one should not borrow from someone who needs the money himself.

WERNER: Of yes, that's me alright! What do I need it for, then? . . . Whoever has need of a sergeant-major will give him enough to live on.

TELLHEIM: You want to become something better than a sergeant-major; to move along a way that's barred to even the best if they've no money.

WERNER: Better than a sergeant-major? I've no thoughts of that. I'm a good sergeant-major; I might easily turn out a bad captain, and certainly a worse general. We've had experience of that.

TELLHEIM: Don't let me think something unjust of you, Werner! I was unhappy to hear what Just told me. You have sold your farm and intend to go off roaming again.

Don't lead me to believe that it's not the profession you love so much as the wild and dissolute way of life that unfortunately goes with it. One should be a soldier for one's country, or out of love for the cause for which one is fighting. To serve here today and there tomorrow, with no aim in view; that's no better than being a travelling butcher, nothing more.

WERNER: Very well, then; I'll take your advice. You know best what's right. I'll stay with you. . . . But in the meantime, Major, take my money. Today or tomorrow your affairs must be settled. You'll get heaps of gold. Then you can give it back to me with interest. I'm only doing it for the interest.

TELLHEIM: Not another word about it.

WERNER: My God, I'm only doing it for the sake of the interest! . . . Sometimes I think to myself: How's it going to be when I'm old and cut to bits? When I'll have nothing? When I'll have to go begging? Then I think to myself: No, I won't have to go begging; I'll go to Major Tellheim; he'll share his last Pfennig with me; he'll look after me till I die; with him I'll be able to die an honest man.

TELLHEIM: *(Taking his hand.)* And, Comrade, you no longer think that?

WERNER: No, I no longer think that. . . . The man who won't take from me what I have, when he's in need, won't give me what he has, when I'm in need. . . . All right, then! *(Makes to go.)*

TELLHEIM: Don't make me angry, man! Where do you think you're going? *(Restrains him.)* If I swear to you now, on my honour, that I have money still. If I promise you, on my honour, that I will tell you when I have none left; that you will be the first, and only person from whom I will borrow. Now are you satisfied?

WERNER: I suppose so. . . . Give me your hand on it, Major.

TELLHEIM: There, Paul! . . . And now, no more of this. I came here to speak with a certain maid . . .

SCENE EIGHT

Franziska (from Minna's rooms), Von Tellheim, Paul Werner.

FRANZISKA: *(Entering)* Are you still here, Sergeant-Major? . . . *(Sees Tellheim.)* and you here too, Major? . . . I'll be at your service in just a moment.

Exit quickly into Minna's rooms again.

SCENE NINE

Von Tellheim, Paul Werner.

TELLHEIM: That's her! . . . but I see you know her, Werner?

WERNER: Yes, I know the little lady . . .

TELLHEIM: But, if I remember rightly, you weren't with me in winter quarters in Thuringia?

WERNER: No, I was in Leipzig collecting equipment.

TELLHEIM: How do you come to know her, then?

WERNER: Our acquaintance is quite a new one. It only started today. But new friendships are warm.

TELLHEIM: And I suppose you've also seen the Fräulein, her mistress?

WERNER: Is her Ladyship a Fräulein? She told me you knew her Ladyship.

TELLHEIM: Yes, didn't you know? She's from Thuringia.

WERNER: Is the Fräulein young?

TELLHEIM: Yes.

WERNER: Beautiful?

TELLHEIM: Very beautiful.

WERNER: Rich?

TELLHEIM: Very rich.

WERNER: And does the Fräulein like you as much as the maid
            does? That would be splendid!

TELLHEIM: What do you mean?

SCENE TEN

Franziska (with a letter in her hand), Von Tellheim, Paul Werner.

FRANZISKA: Herr Major . . .

TELLHEIM: My dear Franziska, I have not yet had a chance to bid
            you welcome.

FRANZISKA: I dare say you have done it in thought. I know you like
            me. And I like you. But it's not very nice to frighten
            people like that, if you like them.

WERNER: *(Aside)* Now I see. It's true!

TELLHEIM: What's my fate, Franziska? . . . Did you give her the
            letter?

FRANZISKA: And I'm to give you here . . . *(Offers him the letter.)*

TELLHEIM: A reply?

FRANZISKA: No, your own letter back again.

TELLHEIM: What? Will she not read it?

FRANZISKA: She wanted to certainly, but . . . we're not good at
            reading handwriting.

TELLHEIM: Very witty!

FRANZISKA: And we think that letter writing was not invented for
            people who can speak to each other face to face
            whenever they like.

TELLHEIM: What sort of an excuse is that? She must read it. It
            contains my justification . . . all the grounds and
            reasons . . .

FRANZISKA: Which my Lady will not read, but will hear from you
            in person.

TELLHEIM: From me in person? So that her every word and look
            can confuse me, and I can read in her every glance the
            magnitude of my loss? . . .

FRANZISKA: Without mercy! . . . Take it *(Gives him the letter.)* She will expect you at three o'clock. She wishes to go for a drive to see the city. You are to accompany her.

TELLHEIM: Accompany her?

FRANZISKA: And what will you give me to let you two go out driving all by yourselves? I'll stay at home.

TELLHEIM: By ourselves?

FRANZISKA: In a pretty, closed carriage.

TELLHEIM: That's not possible!

FRANZISKA: Oh yes it is! In the carriage the Major will have to stand his ground. He won't be able to give us the slip. That's why. . . . In short, you're coming, Major. And at three on the dot. . . . Now, you wanted to see me alone too. Well, what have you got to say, then? Oh, I see we're not alone. *(Looks at Werner.)*

TELLHEIM: Yes, Franziska, as good as alone. But as her Ladyship has not read the letter, I have nothing more to say to you.

FRANZISKA: So, as good as alone, are we? You have no secrets from the Sergeant-Major?

TELLHEIM: No, none.

FRANZISKA: Still, it seems to me, you should keep some things from him.

TELLHEIM: How so?

WERNER: Why's that, Little Lady?

FRANZISKA: Especially secrets of a particular kind. . . . All twenty, Sergeant-Major? *(Holds up her hand with outspread fingers.)*

WERNER: Shush! Little Lady!

TELLHEIM: What does she mean?

FRANZISKA: Quick as a flash, it's on your finger, Sergeant-Major? *(Pretends to put a ring on her finger.)*

TELLHEIM: What's all this about?

WERNER: Little Lady, can't you take a joke?

TELLHEIM: Werner, I hope you've not forgotten what I've told you often enough: not to take a joke with a lady past a certain point?

WERNER: Upon my soul, I may have forgotten! . . . Little Lady, I beg you . . .

FRANZISKA: Well, if it *was* a joke, I'll forgive him this once.

TELLHEIM: If I really must come, Franziska, would you at least make sure that her Ladyship has read my letter beforehand? That will spare me the pain of thinking and speaking once more of things which I would so gladly forget. There, give it to her! *(As he turns the letter over and goes to give it to her, he notices that it has been opened.)* But what's this? The letter has been opened.

FRANZISKA: You could be right. *(Looks at him.)* You are right, it has been opened. But who can have opened it then? No, we really haven't read it, Major, really. Nor do we want to read it, for the writer is coming in person. Please come; and you know what, Major? Don't come like that, like you look now, in boots, with your hair all over the place. We forgive you now; you weren't expecting us. But come in shoes, with your hair dressed. . . . You look too military, too Prussian for me like that!

TELLHEIM: Thank you, Franziska.

FRANZISKA: You look as if you camped out last night.

TELLHEIM: You're not far wrong.

FRANZISKA: We'll spruce ourselves up as well, and then eat lunch. We would like to ask you to stay for lunch, but your presence might upset our eating, and you see, we're not so much in love that we've lost our appetite.

TELLHEIM: I'm going! Franziska, would you prepare her a little for me, so that I don't appear contemptible either in her eyes or my own. . . . Come, Werner, you shall eat with me.

WERNER: At a table in this inn? I wouldn't enjoy a single mouthful.

TELLHEIM: No, with me at my rooms.

WERNER: Then I'll follow you directly. I just want a word with
          the little lady.

TELLHEIM: That's fine by me!

          Exit.

SCENE ELEVEN

Paul Werner, Franziska.

FRANZISKA: Well, Sergeant-Major? . . .

WERNER: Little Lady, when I come back, would you like me
          spruced up as well?

FRANZISKA: Come as you like, Sergeant-Major, my eyes won't find
          fault with you. But my ears will be all the more on
          their guard against you. . . . Twenty fingers, and a ring
          on each one! Well, well, Sergeant-Major!

WERNER: No, that's what I wanted to say to you, Little Lady. I
          got a bit carried away there! There's nothing to that.
          One ring is quite enough. And a hundred and one
          times I've heard the Major say: 'A soldier must be a
          louse to lead a girl on' . . . And I feel the same, Little
          Lady. You can count on that! . . . I must go and catch
          him up. . . . Enjoy your lunch, Little Lady!

          Exit.

FRANZISKA: The same to you, Sergeant-Major! . . . I think I rather
          like that man!

          As she makes to leave she meets Minna.

SCENE TWELVE

Minna, Franziska.

MINNA: Has the Major gone already? . . . Franziska, I think I
          would have been calm enough now to have asked him
          to lunch.

FRANZISKA: And I'll make you calmer still.

MINNA: All the better! His letter, oh, his letter! Every line set
               forth the honesty, the nobility of the man. Every
               hesitation to accept me made his love more dear to
               me. . . . I suppose he saw we had read his letter . . . let
               him, as long as he is prepared to come. He is coming
               for certain? . . . It seems to me, Franziska, there is just
               a little too much pride in his conduct. For being
               unwilling to owe his good fortune to his beloved is
               pride, unpardonable pride! If I see this too strongly in
               him, Franziska . . .

FRANZISKA: You'll renounce him?

MINNA: Come now, Franziska! Don't you pity him any longer?
               No, my dear little fool, one doesn't renounce a man on
               account of a single failing. No. But I have thought of a
               plan to tease him about his pride by showing him a
               little of our own.

FRANZISKA: Well, my Lady, you must truly be calm again, if you
               can plan such tricks.

MINNA: And so I am. Come now. You will have your part to
               play in it too.

               Exeunt.

               END OF ACT THREE

ACT FOUR

SCENE ONE

The Lady's room.

Minna, (richly but tastefully dressed) and Franziska are rising from the table, which a servant is clearing.

FRANZISKA: You can't have finished, Madam.

MINNA: Do you think so, Franziska? Perhaps I was not hungry when I sat down.

FRANZISKA: We may have agreed not to mention him while we were eating, but we should really have made up our minds not even to think about him.

MINNA: You're right. I have thought of nothing else.

FRANZISKA: I could see that well enough. I began talking of a hundred different things, but I didn't get a proper response to any of them. *(Another servant brings in coffee.)* Here comes a drink to match your low spirits: Dear melancholy coffee!

MINNA: Low spirits? Not at all. I am just thinking over the lesson I am going to teach him. You did understand, Franziska?

FRANZISKA: Oh yes, but how much better it would have been if he'd spared us the need to teach him one.

MINNA: You will see that I know him through and through. The man who will reject me now, with all my wealth, will move heaven and earth for me as soon as he hears that I am forsaken and in distress.

FRANZISKA: *(Very earnest.)* That should satisfy the most refined self-esteem!

MINNA: You little moraliser! Look! One minute you're reproving me for my vanity, the next for my self-esteem. . . . Well, just leave me alone, Franziska. You may do as you please with your sergeant-major.

FRANZISKA: With my sergeant-major?

MINNA: Yes, however you may seek to deny it, it's still true . . .
              I have yet to see him, but from every word you have
              spoken about him, I prophesy you a husband.

SCENE TWO

Riccaut de la Marlinière, Minna, Franziska.

RICCAUT: *(Off)* Est-il permis, Monsieur le Major?

FRANZISKA: What's that? Is that for us? *(Goes to the door.)*

RICCAUT: Parbleu! I am not right. . . . Mais non. . . . I am not
              wrong. . . . C'est sa chambre.

FRANZISKA: I see, Madam. This gentleman thought to find Major
              von Tellheim still here.

RICCAUT: Is so. . . . Le Major von Tellheim. Juste, ma belle
              enfant, c'est lui que je cherche. Où est-il?

FRANZISKA: He doesn't live here any more.

RICCAUT: Comment? He lodge here still twenty-four hour ago?
              He lodge no more here? Where he lodge then?

MINNA: Mein Herr . . . *(Approaching him.)*

RICCAUT: Ah, Madam . . . Mademoiselle . . . Your Grace, forgive
              . . .

MINNA: Mein Herr, your mistake is easily forgiven, and your
              surprise very natural. The Major has had the goodness
              to surrender his room to me, a stranger who could not
              find lodgings.

RICCAUT: Ah, voilà de ses politesses! C'est un très-galant-homme
              que ce Major!

MINNA: But where he has moved to . . . indeed, I am ashamed
              to say I do not know.

RICCAUT: Your Grace not know? C'est dommage; j'en suis fâché.

MINNA: I really ought to have made enquiries. For, of course,
              his friends will come here for him.

RICCAUT: I am very of his friend, your Grace . . .

MINNA: Franziska, do you not know?

FRANZISKA: No, Madam.

RICCAUT: I have to speak him most important. I come bring him
            news make him very happy.

MINNA: I regret it all the more. But I have hopes of speaking
            with him, perhaps soon. If it is all one from whose
            mouth he hears this good news, then I will offer, Mein
            Herr . . .

RICCAUT: Understand . . . Mademoiselle, parle français? Mais
            sans doute; tel que je la vois! . . . Le demande était
            bien impolie; vous me pardonnerez, Mademoiselle.

MINNA: Mein Herr . . .

RICCAUT: No? You speak not French, your Grace?

MINNA: Mein, Herr, I would try to speak it in France. But why
            here? I can see that you understand me, mein Herr.
            And I, mein Herr, will most certainly understand you.
            Speak as you like best.

RICCAUT: Good, good! I can explain myself in German also . . .
            Sachez donc, Mademoiselle. . . . Your Grace should
            know then that I come from the table of the Minister
            . . . Minister of . . . Minister of . . . how you call the
            Minister out there? On the long street? . . . on the big
            square?

MINNA: I am, myself, a complete stranger here still.

RICCAUT: Well then, the Minister of the War Department . . . I
            lunched there today . . . I lunch with him mostly . . .
            and the talk came to Major Tellheim. Et le ministre m'a
            dit en confidence, car Son Excellence est de mes amis,
            et il n'y a point de mystères entre nous . . . His
            Excellency, I mean to say, have confide me that the
            affair of our Major is on the point of ending. He has
            maked a report to the King, and the King has resolved
            on it, tout-à-fait en faveur du Major . . . Monsieur, m'a
            dit Son Excellence, vous comprenez bien, que tout
            dépend de la manière, dont on fait envisager les choses
            au Roi, et vous me connaissez. Cela fait un très-joli
            garçon que ce Tellheim, et ne sais-je pas que vous

l'aimez? Les amis des mes amis sont aussi les miens. Il coute un peu cher au Roi ce Tellheim, mais est-ce que l'on sert les rois pour rien? Il faut s'entr'aider en ce monde; et quand il s'agit de pertes, que ce soit le Roi, qui en fasse, et non pas un honnête homme de nous autres. Voilà le principe, dont je ne me dépars jamais. . . . What say your Grace to that? He is a fine man, no? Ah que Son Excellence a le coeur bien placé! He has assured me that if the Major has not already received a letter . . . a letter from the King's hand, that he must infallibly receive one today.

MINNA: Indeed mein Herr, this news will prove very agreeable to Major von Tellheim. I would wish only to be able to name to him the friend who was taken such an interest in his good fortune. . .

RICCAUT: You wish my name, Your Grace? . . . Vous voyez en moi . . . Your Grace see in me le Chevalier Riccaut de la Marlinière, Seigneur de Prêt-au-vol, de la Branche de Prensd'or . . . Your Grace is amazed to hear that I am from such a great, great family, which is certainly of the royal blood . . . Il faut le dire; je suis sans doute le cadet le plus aventureux, que la maison a jamais eu . . . I am serving since I am eleven years. An affair d'honneur is making me fly. Since then I am serving His Holiness the Pope, the Republic of San Marino, the crown of Poland, and the States-General, until I am finding myself here at last. Ah, Mademoiselle, que je voudrais, n'avoir jamais vu ce pays-là! If they were leaving me in the service of the States-General, then I am being at least the colonel. But here for ever and ever the capitaine, and now I am even being the discharged capitaine . . .

MINNA: That is unfortunate.

RICCAUT: Oui, Mademoiselle, me voilà reformé, et par-là mis sur le pavé!

MINNA: I grieve to hear it.

RICCAUT: Vous êtes bien bonne, Mademoiselle. . . . No, here one do not have one's true reward. To demobilate a man like me! . . . A man who has ruinised himself in their service! . . . More also, I am sacrificing more than

twenty thousand livres. What have I now? Tranchons le
mot; je n'ai pas le sou, et me voilà exactement vis-à-vis
du rien.

MINNA: I am extremely sorry.

RICCAUT: Vous êtes bien bonne, Mademoiselle. But as people say:
            every misfortune he bring his brother; qu'un malheur
            ne vient jamais seul. So it arrive to me. An honnet-
            homme of my extraction, what other resource can he
            have but the cards? Well now, I have always played
            with the luck, so long I don't need her. Now I need
            her, Mademoiselle, je joue avec un guignon, qui
            surpasse toute croyance. Since fifteen days, not one
            when she has not broke my bank. Yesterday too she
            break me three times. Je sais bien, qu'il y avait quelque
            chose de plus que le jeu. Car parmi mes pontes se
            trouvaient certaines dames. . . . I will say no more. One
            must be gallant to the ladies. They have invite me
            today also to give me my revenge, mais . . . vous
            m'entendez, Mademoiselle. . . . First one must have
            money to live before one can have money to play . . .

MINNA: I hope, Sir . . .

RICCAUT: Vous êtes bien bonne, Mademoiselle . . .

MINNA: (Taking Franziska aside.) Franziska, I feel genuinely
            moved by the man. Do you think he would take it
            amiss if I were to offer him something?

FRANZISKA: He doesn't look like that sort to me.

MINNA: Good! . . . Mein Herr, I hear . . . that you play, that
            you keep bank, no doubt in places where there is
            something to be won. I must confess to you that I . . .
            I too greatly love cards . . .

RICCAUT: Tant mieux, Mademoiselle, tant mieux! Tous les gens
            d'esprit aiment le jeu à la fureur.

MINNA: That I am fond of winning, and that I am keen to
            venture my money with a man who . . . knows how to
            play. Would you be inclined, mein Herr, to take me
            into partnership with you? To grant me a share in your
            bank?

RICCAUT: Comment, Mademoiselle, vous voulez être de moitié avec moi? De tout mon coeur.

MINNA: Just a trifle to start with . . . *(Goes and fetches money from her purse.)*

RICCAUT: Ah, Mademoiselle, que vous êtes charmante!

MINNA: I have here something I won only recently, only ten Pistoles. . . . I am quite ashamed. . . . It is so little . . .

RICCAUT: Donnez toujours, Mademoiselle, donnez. *(Takes it.)*

MINNA: Of course, mein Herr, your bank is most respectable . . .

RICCAUT: Oh yes, most respectable. Ten Pistoles. For that your Grace shall have an interest in my bank the third, pour le tiers. For a third there should really be . . . a little more. But with a beautiful lady, one must not split the hairs. I congratulate me to have come in connection with your Grace, et de ce moment je recommence à bien augurer de ma fortune.

MINNA: I fear I can not be present while you play, mein Herr.

RICCAUT: What needs your Grace be there? We card players are men of honour.

MINNA: If we are not fortunate, mein Herr, will you bring me my share; and if we are unfortunate . . .

RICCAUT: Then I come to fetch the new recruits, no, your Grace?

MINNA: By and by the recruits may run short. So defend our money bravely, mein Herr.

RICCAUT: What for you take me, your Grace? A dunderhead? A Simple Simon?

MINNA: Forgive me . . .

RICCAUT: Je suis de bons, Mademoiselle. Savez-vous ce que cela veut dire? I have the experience . . .

MINNA: But still, mein Herr . . .

RICCAUT: Je sais monter un coup . . .

MINNA: *(Surprised)* But should you?

RICCAUT: Je file la carte avec une adresse . . .

MINNA: Never!

RICCAUT: Je fais sauter la coupe avec une dexterité . . .

MINNA: But you will not all the same, mein Herr . . .

RICCAUT: Why not, your Grace, why not? Donnez-moi un
             pigeonneau à plumer, et . . .

MINNA: Play false? Cheat?

RICCAUT: Comment, Mademoiselle? Vous appelez cela cheating?
             Corriger la fortune, l'enchâiner sous les doigts, être sûr
             de son fait, that the Germans call cheating? Cheating?
             Oh, the German language she is so poor! So clumsy!

MINNA: No Sir, if you think that . . .

RICCAUT: Laissez-moi faire, Mademoiselle, and stay calm! What
             matter you how I play? . . . enough; tomorrow you see
             me again with hundred Pistoles, or your Grace not see
             me again. . . . Votre très-humble, Mademoiselle, votre
             très-humble . . .

                    Exit hurriedly.

MINNA: *(Looking after him in astonishment.)* I hope, mein Herr,
             it will be the latter!

SCENE THREE

Minna, Franziska.

FRANZISKA: *(Bitterly)* May I speak now? Oh, well done! Well done!

MINNA: Mock me, I deserve it. *(After a moment's thought, more
             composed.)* No, do not mock me. Franziska, I do not
             deserve it.

FRANZISKA: Splendid! Well, now you've done something really
             worthwhile: put a swindler back on his feet again.

MINNA: I intended helping a man down on his luck.

FRANZISKA: And the best of it is that the lout took you for one of
             his own kind. . . . I must go after him and get your
             money back.

MINNA: Franziska, don't let the coffee get quite cold; pour it out.

FRANZISKA: He must return it to you; you have thought better of it; you do not wish to partner him at the table. Ten Pistoles! Surely you could see he was a beggar, Madam! *(Minna pours coffee herself.)* And who'd give that much to a beggar? Then even to spare him the indignity of having to beg for it? Beggars usually forget the kindhearted people, who in their generosity fail to recognise them as such. But it would serve you right if he sees your gift as . . . as . . . well, I don't know what. *(Minna hands Franziska a cup.)* Do you really want to make my blood boil? I won't drink it. *(Minna puts it down.)* . . . 'Parbleu, your Grace, here one do not have one's true reward'. *(Impersonating)* Quite true, if they let rogues like him run around without hanging them.

MINNA: *(Cool and thoughtful, drinking.)* My girl, you are so very good at understanding good people; but when will you learn to cope with the bad ones . . . for they are people too . . . and frequently not half so bad as they appear. . . . One has only to look for their good side. I fancy this Frenchman is simply vain. Out of sheer vanity he makes himself out a cheat; he does not wish to be obliged to me; to have to thank me. Perhaps he will go away now, pay off his small debts, and live quietly and frugally on the remainder as long as it lasts, and think no more of gaming. If so, my dear Franziska, he may come and fetch fresh recruits as often as he likes. . . . *(Gives her the cup.)* There, clear away. . . But tell me, should not Tellheim be here by now?

FRANZISKA: No, my Lady; I just can't do it; I can't see the good side in a bad person, nor the bad side in a good one.

MINNA: But he *is* coming?

FRANZISKA: Just let him stay away! . . . You see in him, in him the best of men, a little pride, and for that you are going to tease him so cruelly?

MINNA: Are you coming back to that? . . . Enough! I will, just this once. And if you spoil this game for me; if you do not say and do everything as we agreed! . . . Well then,

I'll leave you alone with him, and then . . . But here
he is . . .

SCENE FOUR

Paul Werner, stiffly, as if on parade. Minna, Franziska.

FRANZISKA: No, it's only his dear sergeant-major.

MINNA: Dear sergeant-major? Who's the 'dear' for?

FRANZISKA: Madam, please don't embarrass the gentleman. . . .
Your servant, Sergeant-Major. What have you got for
us?

WERNER: *(Taking no notice of Franziska, approaches Minna.)* Major
von Tellheim commands me, Sergeant-Major Werner,
to convey to your Ladyship his humble respects, and to
say that he will be here without delay.

MINNA: What's keeping him?

WERNER: Your pardon, my Lady. We did leave his lodgings
before three o'clock struck, but he was accosted on the
way by the Army Paymaster; and as there's no getting
away from that sort of gentleman, he gave me a nod to
inform you of the occurrence.

MINNA: Very good, Sergeant-Major. I only hope that the
Paymaster may have something pleasant to say to the
Major.

WERNER: They seldom have for the officers these days. . . . Has
your Ladyship any further orders? *(Makes to go.)*

FRANZISKA: Well now, where are you off to, Sergeant-Major?
Haven't you and I got some talking to do?

WERNER: *(Softly and seriously to Franziska.)* Not here, Little
Lady. It's not respectful, it's not fitting. . . . Your
Ladyship . . .

MINNA: I thank you for your trouble, Sergeant-Major. . . . I am
pleased to have made your acquaintance. Franziska has
spoken to me very highly of you.

Werner bows stiffly and exit.

SCENE FIVE

Minna, Franziska.

MINNA: So that is your sergeant-major, Franziska?

FRANZISKA: I haven't time to take exception to your mockery. . . .
              Yes, my Lady, that is 'my' sergeant-major. You, no
              doubt, find him a little stiff and wooden. I almost
              thought so myself this time. But I know why. He felt
              he had to put on his parade manners in front of you,
              your Ladyship. And when they are on parade . . .
              soldiers *do* look more like puppets than men. But you
              ought to see him, and hear him, when he's left to
              himself!

MINNA: Perhaps I should!

FRANZISKA: He'll be downstairs still. Can't I go down and have a
              little chat with him now?

MINNA: I don't like having to deny you this pleasure, but you
              must remain here, Franziska. You must be present at
              our interview! . . . I've had another idea. *(Takes her
              ring from her finger.)* Here, take my ring; you take care
              of it, and give me the Major's in its place.

FRANZISKA: Whatever for?

MINNA: *(While Franziska fetches the other ring.)* I don't quite
              know myself yet, but I fancy I can see a way in which
              I might use it. . . . Someone's knocking. . . . Quickly,
              give it to me! *(Puts it on.)* It's him!

SCENE SIX

*Von Tellheim (dressed the same, but otherwise as Franziska requested),
Minna, Franziska.*

TELLHEIM: My Lady, pray forgive my delay . . .

MINNA: Oh, Major, not so military with me, if you please. So
              here you are! And to await a pleasure is a pleasure in
              itself. . . . Well? *(Looks at him smilingly.)* My dear
              Tellheim, haven't we been children?

TELLHEIM: Yes, children indeed, my Lady, resisting when they should patiently submit.

MINNA: We are going for a drive, my dear Major . . . to see something of the city . . . and afterwards to meet my uncle.

TELLHEIM: What?

MINNA: You see, we haven't had the opportunity to discuss the most important matter. Yes, he is arriving here today. An accident meant that I arrived a day ahead of him.

TELLHEIM: Count von Bruchsall? Is he back?

MINNA: The upheavals of the war drove him into Italy; but the peace has summoned him back again. . . . Don't worry, Tellheim. If at one time we expected the strongest opposition to our union to come from him . . .

TELLHEIM: Our union?

MINNA: He is your friend. He has heard too many good reports of you from too many people to be anything else. He is eager to meet face to face the man who is the choice of his sole heiress. He is coming as an uncle, a guardian, as a father to give me to you.

TELLHEIM: Ah, Fräulein, why did you not read my letter? Why did you refuse to read it?

MINNA: Your letter? Oh yes, I remember, you sent me one. What happened to the letter, Franziska? Did we read it, or did we not read it? Well, my dear Tellheim, what did you write to me?

TELLHEIM: Nothing but what my honour commanded.

MINNA: Which is not to leave a lady of honour, whom you love, in the lurch. I have no doubt that is what your honour commands. Indeed, I should have read your letter. But what I didn't read, I can hear from you now.

TELLHEIM: Yes, you *shall* hear it . . .

MINNA: No, I have no need to hear it. It's all too obvious. That you are capable of dealing me the cruellest of blows in saying you no longer want me. Are you not aware that for the rest of my life my country-women will point

their fingers at me and say: 'That's her; that's Fräulein
von Barnhelm, who imagined that, because she was
rich, she could win the gallant Tellheim; as if the
gallant man could be had for money!' That is what they
will say, for my country-women are all envious of me.
That I am rich, they cannot deny; but what they refuse
to accept is that I am really quite a good girl, and one
worthy of her husband. Is that not so, Tellheim?

TELLHEIM: Oh yes, my Lady, I recognise your country-women in
that. They will have every reason to envy you your
discharged officer, dishonoured, a cripple and a beggar.

MINNA: And are you all of those? I heard something of the kind
only this morning, if I was not mistaken. But there may
be both good and bad in this. Let us investigate each
point more closely. . . . You are discharged, are you?
So you said. I thought that your regiment had simply
been redeployed. How does it happen that they have
not retained a man of your merit?

TELLHEIM: It has happened as it must happen. The great have
decided that a soldier will do very little out of fondness
for them; not a great deal more out of a sense of duty;
but anything for the sake of his own honour. Why,
then, should they think themselves in his debt? The
peace has allowed them to dispense with any number of
my kind; and in the end, they find nobody
indispensable.

MINNA: You speak like a man who, for his part, finds the great
equally dispensable. And never more so than at this
moment. I offer the great my heartfelt thanks that they
have renounced their claims on a man whom I only
very unwillingly shared with them in the first
place. . . . I am your commander, Tellheim; you need
no other master. . . . To find you discharged, I hardly
dared dream of such good fortune! . . . But you are not
simply discharged; there is more. And what more? A
cripple, you say? Well, *(Taking a good look at him.)* this
cripple is pretty sound and able-bodied as yet, and
seems pretty hale and hearty to me still. . . . My dear
Tellheim, if you are proposing to go begging on the
strength of the loss of your sound limbs, I prophesy

now that you find pity at very few doors, except at
those of kind hearted girls like me.

TELLHEIM: In all this I can hear nothing but a mischievous girl,
dear Minna.

MINNA: And in your rebuke I hear nothing but the 'dear
Minna' . . . I will stop my mischief. For I suppose you
are something of a cripple, after all. A shot has slightly
lamed your right hand. . . . But, all things considered,
that's none too bad either. You're less likely to hit
me.

TELLHEIM: Fräulein!

MINNA: You're going to say that I am more likely to hit you
now? Well, well, my dear Tellheim, I hope you will not
let it come to that.

TELLHEIM: You are determined to laugh, mein Fräulein. I am only
sorry that I cannot laugh with you.

MINNA: Why ever not? What do you have against laughter?
Can one laugh and be serious at the same time? My
dear Major, laughter preserves our reason better than
ill-humour. We have the proof before us. Your
laughing friend judges your circumstances far more
fairly than you do yourself. You have been discharged,
and you say your honour has been offended. You have
been shot in the arm, and you say you are a cripple!
Now is that correct, or is that exaggeration? And
haven't I always subjected exaggeration to ridicule like
this? I'll wager that if I put your beggary to the test, it
would not stand scrutiny either. You may have lost
your kit once, twice or three times; some deposits with
some banker or other may have vanished; you may
have no hope of recovering this or that advance which
you made in the service; but are you on that account a
beggar? If you had nothing more than my uncle is
bringing you . . .

TELLHEIM: Your uncle, my Lady, will be bringing me nothing.

MINNA: Nothing but the two thousand Pistoles you so
generously advanced to our estates.

TELLHEIM: If you had only read my letter, my Lady!

MINNA: All right, I did read it. But what I read there on this
              matter was a complete puzzle to me. They can't wish to
              make a noble action out to be a crime . . . please
              explain, my dear Major.

TELLHEIM: You remember, my Lady, that I was under orders to
              collect the war levy in your district in cash, and with
              the utmost severity. Wishing to avoid this severity, I
              advanced the sum required myself.

MINNA: Indeed I remember that. I loved you for this act, even
              before I first saw you.

TELLHEIM: The estates gave me their bill, which I intended to
              register among the debts to be settled, as soon as peace
              had been signed. The bill was acknowledged as valid,
              but my claim in it was contested. They sneered in
              derision when I assured them that I had provided the
              sum in cash. They saw it as a bribe, a reward from the
              estates for my having so readily agreed with them on
              the smallest sum which I had authority to accept. Thus
              it was that the bill left my possession, and when it is
              paid, it is certain that it will not be paid to me. . . . It
              is on this account that I regard my honour as offended;
              not my discharge, which I would have asked for myself,
              had I not received it. . . . You look serious, my Lady?
              Why are you not laughing? Ha, ha, ha! Look, I'm
              laughing.

MINNA: Oh, stifle this laughter, Tellheim! I implore you! It is a
              terrifying laughter which betrays a hatred of humanity!
              No, you are not a man to regret a good deed because it
              has evil consequences for you. No, these evil
              consequences cannot last. The truth must come to
              light. The testimony of my uncle, of all our estates. . . .

TELLHEIM: Your uncle! Your estates! Ha, ha, ha!

MINNA: Your laughter will kill me, Tellheim! If you have any
              faith in virtue and providence, Tellheim, do not laugh
              like that. I have heard no more terrible cursing than
              this laughter of yours. . . . Let us suppose the very
              worst. If they are all determined to misrepresent you
              here, still they cannot misrepresent you to us. No, we
              cannot, we will not misunderstand you, Tellheim. And
              if our estates have even the slightest sense of honour, I

know what they must do. But how stupid of me. Why
does it matter what they do? Just imagine. Tellheim,
that you had lost the two thousand Pistoles on some
wild night out. The King may have been an unlucky
card for you; well, the Queen *(Pointing to herself.)* will
be all the kinder to you for that. . . . Providence,
believe me, will always save an honest man from
harm; often in advance. The action which at one time
was to cost you two thousand Pistoles, won me for you.
But for this action, I would not have been so eager to
make your acquaintance. You know that I came,
without an invitation, to the first function where I
thought I might find you. I came solely on your
account. I came with the firm intention of loving
you. . . . I loved you already with the firm intention of
making you mine, even if I had found you as black and
ugly as the Moor of Venice. And you are not so black,
nor so ugly; nor will you be so jealous. But Tellheim,
Tellheim, you do have much in common with him! Oh,
these savage inflexible men, who forever fix their
staring eyes on the spectres of their honour! And steel
themselves against all other feelings! . . . Turn your
eyes this way! On me, Tellheim! *(He looks motionless
and absorbed away from her.)* What are you thinking?
Can you not hear me?

TELLHEIM: *(Distractedly)* Oh yes! But tell me, my Lady, how did
the Moor come to be in the Venetian service? Had this
Moor no country of his own? Why did he hire out his
arm and his blood to a foreign state?

MINNA: *(Terrified)* Where are you, Tellheim? . . . It's time we
broke off our conversation. . . . Come! *(Takes him by the
hand.)* Franziska, call the carriage.

TELLHEIM: *(Tearing himself away from Minna, and going to
Franziska.)* No, Franziska, I cannot have the honour of
accompanying her Ladyship. . . . My Lady, let me
retain my senses for today at least, and permit me to
withdraw. You are going the right way to deprive me of
them. I am resisting, as best I can. . . . And while I am
still in possession of my reason, listen to what I have
firmly resolved, my Lady, and from which nothing in
the world will deflect me. . . . If there are no more

lucky throws left for me in the game, if the tide does
not turn for me . . . if . . .

MINNA: I must interrupt you, Major. . . . We should have told
              him straight away, Franziska. Why do you never
              remind me of anything? . . . Our conversation would
              have taken quite another route, had I started with the
              good news which the Chevalier de la Marlinière came to
              bring you just now.

TELLHEIM: The Chevalier de la Marlinière? Who is he?

FRANZISKA: He might be a good man, Major, but for . . .

MINNA: Silence, Franziska. . . . Like you, he is a discharged
              officer, of the Dutch service . . .

TELLHEIM: Ah, Lieutenant Riccaut!

MINNA: He assured me he was your friend.

TELLHEIM: And I assure you I am not his.

MINNA: And that, I don't know which minister had confided in
              him that your affair was nearing a happy conclusion. A
              letter from the King must be on its way to you . . .

TELLHEIM: How should Riccaut and a minister come to meet? . . .
              But something must indeed have happened in my case,
              for just now the Army Paymaster explained to me that
              the King had quashed everything which had been
              alleged against me, and that I could withdraw my
              written word of honour not to leave here until I had
              been fully exonerated. . . . But that will be all. They
              will allow me to run away. But they are mistaken; I will
              not run. I would rather waste away in the depths of
              misery before the eyes of my slanderers . . .

MINNA: You stiff-necked man! . . .

TELLHEIM: I have no use for a pardon; I want justice. My
              honour . . .

MINNA: The honour of a man like you . . .

TELLHEIM: (Heatedly) You may well be a good judge of many
              things, but not in this case. Honour is not the voice of
              our own conscience, nor the testimony of a few right-
              minded . . .

MINNA: No, no. I am aware that . . . honour is . . . honour.

TELLHEIM: In short, my Lady. . . . You did not permit me to
            finish. . . . I intended to say that if they so
            disgracefully withhold what is mine, and if I do not
            receive complete satisfaction for my honour, I cannot
            be yours, my Lady, for I would not be worthy to be so
            in the eyes of the world. Fräulein von Barnhelm
            deserves a husband beyond reproach. It is a worthless
            love which does not scruple to expose its object to
            scorn. It is a worthless man who is not ashamed to owe
            all his good fortune to a woman, whose blind
            tenderness . . .

MINNA: Are you serious, Major? . . . *(Suddenly turns her back on
            him.)* Franziska!

TELLHEIM: Do not be angry, my Lady . . .

MINNA: *(Aside to Franziska.)* Now would be the time! What's
            your advice, Franziska?

FRANZISKA: I can't advise you, but he is rather making a meal of it.

TELLHEIM: *(Coming to interrupt them.)* You are angry, my Lady . . .

MINNA: *(Scornfully)* I? Not in the least.

TELLHEIM: If I loved you less, my Lady . . .

MINNA: *(Same tone.)* That would surely be my misfortune. . . .
            But, equally, Major, I do not wish you misfortune. . . .
            One must be completely unselfish in love. . . . I am
            glad, therefore, that I have not been more open with
            you! Perhaps your pity would have granted me that
            which your love denies me . . . *(Slowly taking the ring
            off her finger.)*

TELLHEIM: What do you mean by that, my Lady?

MINNA: No, neither must make the other either more or less
            fortunate. That is what true love demands! I believe
            you, Major; and your honour is too strong for you to
            fail to recognise true love.

TELLHEIM: Are you mocking me, Madam?

MINNA: Here, take back the ring with which you plighted your

troth to me. *(Offers him the ring.)* So be it! Let it be as
if we had never met!

TELLHEIM: What are you saying?

MINNA: You find this surprising? . . . Take it, Sir. . . . Surely
you were not simply play-acting?

TELLHEIM: *(Taking the ring.)* My God! Can Minna say such
things? . . .

MINNA: In one way you cannot be mine, but in no way can I be
yours. Your misfortune is probable, mine is certain. . . .
Farewell! *(Makes to leave.)*

TELLHEIM: Where are you going, dearest Minna?

MINNA: Sir, you offend me by addressing me in such familiar
terms.

TELLHEIM: What is wrong, my Lady? Where are you going?

MINNA: Leave me . . . that I may conceal my tears from you,
traitor!

Exit.

SCENE SEVEN

Von Tellheim, Franziska.

TELLHEIM: Her tears? And am I to leave her? *(Goes after her.)*

FRANZISKA: *(Restraining him.)* No, no, Major! You are surely not
intending to follow her into her bedroom?

TELLHEIM: Her misfortune? Did she not speak of her misfortune?

FRANZISKA: Certainly! The misfortune of losing you after . . .

TELLHEIM: After? After what? There is more in this. What is it,
Franziska? Tell me, speak . . .

FRANZISKA: I was going to say, after she . . . has sacrificed so much
for you.

TELLHEIM: Sacrificed for me?

FRANZISKA: Just listen a moment. . . . It's a good thing for you to
be rid of her in this way. . . . Why shouldn't I tell you?

It can't remain a secret any longer. . . . We have run away! Count von Bruchsall has disinherited my Lady because she would not marry a husband of his choice. At that she abandoned everything and left home. What were we to do? We decided to seek out the one whom we . . .

TELLHEIM: I have heard enough. . . . Come, I must throw myself at her feet.

FRANZISKA: What can you be thinking of? On the contrary, go away and be grateful for this stroke of luck . . .

TELLHEIM: You wretched girl! What do you take me for? . . . No, my dear Franziska, that advice did not come from your heart. Forgive my anger.

FRANZISKA: Do not detain me. I must see what she is doing. How easily might something happen to her. . . . Go now! . . . Better come another time, if you want to come again, that is.

Exit to Minna.

SCENE EIGHT

Tellheim.

TELLHEIM: But Franziska! . . . I will wait for you here. . . . No, this is more urgent! . . . If she looks at it seriously, she will not be able to refuse me her forgiveness! . . . I have need of you now, honest Werner! . . . no, Minna, I am no traitor.

Exit hurriedly.

END OF ACT FOUR

ACT FIVE

SCENE ONE

The Hall.

Von Tellheim and Werner from opposite sides.

TELLHEIM: Ah, Werner! I've been looking for you everywhere. Where have you been hiding?

WERNER: I've been searching for you, Major . . . well, that's how it goes . . . I've got some good news for you.

TELLHEIM: Oh, I've no use for your news now; I need your money. Quickly, Werner, give me all you have, and then go and raise as much as you can.

WERNER: Major? On my soul, I told you so. He'll borrow from me only when he has money of his own to lend.

TELLHEIM: Surely you're not looking for excuses?

WERNER: To stop me finding fault with him, he takes with his right hand and gives it back with his left.

TELLHEIM: Don't delay me, Werner! I have every intention of returning it to you, but God knows when and how!

WERNER: So you don't know that the State Treasury has orders to pay you your monies? I have just heard from . . .

TELLHEIM: What are you chattering about? What have you let yourself be tricked into believing? Don't you see that, if it were true, I would have been the first to know? . . . Quickly, Werner, money!

WERNER: Well yes, with pleasure! Here's some! . . . Here's the hundred Louis d'Or, and here's the hundred Ducats. *(Gives him both).*

TELLHEIM: Werner, go and take the hundred Louis d'Or to Just. Tell him to redeem the ring at once which he pawned this morning. . . . But where will you get more from, Werner? . . . For I need a great deal more.

WERNER: Let me worry about that. . . . The man who bought my farm lives in the city. The completion date is not for a

fortnight, but the money is ready, and for a half
percent discount . . .

TELLHEIM: Now look, my dear Werner! . . . I am coming to you
alone for help. . . . I must therefore tell you everything.
The lady here . . . you have seen her . . . is in distress
. . .

WERNER: Oh misery!

TELLHEIM: But tomorrow she will be my wife . . .

WERNER: Oh joy!

TELLHEIM: And the day after tomorrow I will leave here with her.
I *can* leave, and I *will* leave. We shall leave things here
to go their own way! Who knows where there may be
some good fortune stored up for me? If you want to,
Werner, why not come with us? Let's enlist again
together.

WERNER: Are you serious? But where's there a war on, Major?

TELLHEIM: There'll be one somewhere. . . . But go now, my dear
Werner; we can talk more about that later.

WERNER: My old Major again! . . . The day after tomorrow?
Why not tomorrow instead? . . . I can get everything
together. . . . In Persia, my dear Major, there's a
splendid war on. What do you say?

TELLHEIM: We'll think about it. Now go on, Werner! . . .

WERNER: Hallelujah! Long live Prince Heraclius!

   Exit.

SCENE TWO

Von Tellheim.

TELLHEIM: What has happened to me? . . . My whole soul has a
new impetus. My own misfortune struck me down. It
made me touchy, short-sighted, timid, sluggish. Her
misfortune has raised me up. I can see about me

clearly, and I feel strong and ready to undertake
anything for her. . . . Why am I waiting?

> *Goes towards Minna's rooms, out of which Franziska
> enters.*

SCENE THREE

Franziska, Von Tellheim.

FRANZISKA: Oh, it's you, then. . . . I thought I heard your
              voice. . . . What do you want, Major?

TELLHEIM: What do I want? . . . What is her Ladyship doing? . . .
              Come here.

FRANZISKA: She is about to go out for a drive.

TELLHEIM: But alone? Without me? Where to?

FRANZISKA: Have you forgotten, Major? . . .

TELLHEIM: Do you not understand, Franziska? . . . I have offended
              her, and she was sensitive to this. I shall beg her for
              forgiveness and she will forgive me.

FRANZISKA: What? . . . after you have taken back the ring, Major?

TELLHEIM: Ah! I was confused when I did that. . . . I have not
              thought of it since. . . . where did I put it? . . . *(Looks
              for it.)* Here it is.

FRANZISKA: Is that it? *(He puts it away.)* *(Aside)* If only he would
              take a closer look!

TELLHEIM: She pressed it on me with a bitterness . . . which I
              have already forgotten. A full heart cannot choose its
              words. . . . But she will not hesitate for a moment to
              take the ring back again. . . . And have I not hers still?

FRANZISKA: Which she will expect in exchange for yours. . . .
              Where is it, then, Major? Let me see it.

TELLHEIM: *(In some confusion.)* I have . . . forgotten to put it
              on. . . . Just . . . Just will fetch it for me at once.

FRANZISKA: Oh, one is much the same as the other. Let me see that
               one. I do love looking at things like that.

TELLHEIM: Another time, Franziska. Come now . . .

FRANZISKA: (*Aside*) He's determined not to see his mistake.

TELLHEIM: What did you say, mistake?

FRANZISKA: It's a mistake, I said, for you to think that my Lady is
               still a good match. Her personal income is far from
               considerable. It's quite possible that her guardians
               might bring it all to nothing in a few selfish deals. All
               her expectations lay with her uncle, but this terrible
               uncle . . .

TELLHEIM: Let him be! . . . Am I not man enough to restore it all
               to her some day?

FRANZISKA: Listen! Her bell! I must go in to her.

TELLHEIM: I will come with you.

FRANZISKA: Heaven forbid! She has expressly forbidden me to
               speak with you! Anyway, come a little behind me, at
               least . . .

               Exit.

SCENE FOUR

Von Tellheim (calling after her.)

TELLHEIM: Announce me! . . . Speak for me, Franziska! . . . I
               will follow you directly. . . . What shall I say to her?
               . . . Where the heart must speak, there is no need to
               prepare. . . . But one thing does demand consideration:
               her reticence, her scruples against throwing herself into
               my arms in her distress, and her determination to
               present a picture of herself still in that good fortune
               which she has lost through me. How can she defend to
               herself her mistrust of my honour and of her worth?
               . . . For my part, I have forgiven her already! . . . Ah!
               Here she is.

SCENE FIVE

Minna, Franziska, Von Tellheim.

MINNA: *(Entering, as if she had not seen Tellheim.)* The carriage
            is at the door, Franziska? . . . My fan!

TELLHEIM: Where are you going, my Lady?

MINNA: *(Affecting coldness.)* Out, Major. . . . Ah, I see why you
            have troubled yourself again. It must be to give me
            your ring back too. . . . Very well, Major; be so good as
            to hand it to Franziska. . . . Franziska, take the ring
            from the Major! . . . I have no time to waste. *(Makes
            to go.)*

TELLHEIM: *(Stepping in front of her.)* My Lady! . . . What I have
            just been told, my Lady! I was not worthy of so much
            love.

MINNA: So, Franziska? You have told the Major . . .

FRANZISKA: Everything.

TELLHEIM: Do not be angry with me, my Lady. I am no traitor.
            You have lost much in the eyes of the world on my
            account, but not in mine. In my eyes you have gained
            immeasurably by this loss. It was too fresh. You were
            afraid that it might make an all too unfavourable
            impression on me. You wanted to conceal it from me at
            first. I am not complaining at your mistrust. It sprang
            from the desire to retain my affection. And this desire
            is my pride! You found me in distress, and you did not
            wish to pile up misfortune on misfortune. You could
            not have guessed how your misfortune would make
            mine seem insignificant.

MINNA: That's all very well, Major. But it is done now. I have
            released you from your obligation; by your taking back
            of the ring you have . . .

TELLHEIM: Consented to nothing! . . . Indeed, I consider myself
            more bound now than before! . . . You are mine,
            Minna, mine forever. *(Takes out ring.)* Here, take this
            for the second time as a pledge of my fidelity . . .

MINNA: I take this ring? This ring?

TELLHEIM: Yes, dearest Minna, yes!

MINNA: What are you asking of me? This ring?

TELLHEIM: You took this ring from my hand for the first time when our circumstances were alike and happy. They are happy no more, but they are, once again, alike. Equality is always the firmest bond of love. . . . Allow me, dearest Minna! . . . *(Takes her hand to put the ring on.)*

MINNA: What? By force, Major? . . . No, there is no force in the world which can compel me to take back this ring! . . . Do you perhaps think I am in need of a ring? . . . You can see well enough that I have here another ring in no way inferior to yours. *(Pointing to her ring.)*

FRANZISKA: He must realise now! . . .

TELLHEIM: *(Letting go of her hand.)* What is this? . . . I see Fraülein von Barnhelm, but I do not hear her voice. . . . You are play-acting, my Lady. . . . Forgive me for repeating your word.

MINNA: *(In her normal tone of voice.)* Did that word offend you?

TELLHEIM: It hurt me.

MINNA: *(Touched)* I did not intend that. Forgive me, Tellheim.

TELLHEIM: Ah, this familiar tone of voice tells me that you are yourself again, my Lady; that you still love me, Minna . . .

FANZISKA: *(Blurting out.)* The joke will go too far in a minute . . .

MINNA: *(Imperiously)* I'll thank you not to interfere in our game, Franziska!

FRANZISKA: *(Taken aback, aside.)* Still not had enough?

MINNA: Yes, Sir, it would be feminine vanity to make myself out cold and scornful. Away with that! You deserve to find me just as sincere as you are yourself. . . . I still love you, Tellheim, I still love you, but notwithstanding that . . .

TELLHEIM: No more, dearest Minna, no more! *(Grasps her hand again, to put on the ring.)*

MINNA: *(Drawing back her hand.)* Notwithstanding that. . . . I
                am all the more determined never to let this happen,
                never! . . . What are you thinking of, Major? . . . I
                would have thought you had enough with your own
                misfortune. . . . You must remain here. You must exact
                the very fullest satisfaction . . . defiantly. For the
                moment I can find no better word . . . defiantly . . .
                even if you should waste away in the depths of misery
                before the eyes of your slanderers.

TELLHEIM: That is what I thought, what I said, when I did not
                know what to think or say. My whole soul was clouded
                over with rage and bitter resentment. Even blessed love
                herself in the fullness of her splendour could not bring
                me daylight in my darkness. But she sent her sister,
                pity, familiar of sad pain, who has dispelled the clouds,
                and has opened all my soul to impressions of
                tenderness. The drive to self-preservation has been re-
                awakened by having something more precious than
                myself to preserve. Do not take offence, my Lady, at
                the word 'pity'. When you are not the cause of your
                own misfortune, you may hear the word without
                humiliation. I am that cause. Through me, Minna, you
                have lost friends and relations, fortune and fatherland.
                Through me and in me, you must find all these again,
                or I will have on my soul the destruction of the finest
                of her sex. Do not make me contemplate a future filled
                with self-hatred. . . . No, nothing will keep me here
                any longer. From this moment I shall counter the
                injustices I have received here with nothing but
                contempt. Is this country the world? Does the sun
                shine nowhere but here? Where might I not go? I
                might take up service anywhere, even under some far-
                off, foreign sky. Follow me with confidence, dearest
                Minna. We shall want for nothing. . . . I have a friend
                who will gladly support me.

SCENE SIX

Dispatch-rider, Von Tellheim, Minna, Franziska.

FRANZISKA: *(Seeing Dispatch-rider)* Psst! Major . . .

TELLHEIM: *(To Dispatch-rider.)* Whom do you want?

DISPATCH- RIDER:	I am looking for Major von Tellheim . . . but that's you, Sir. Herr Major, I am to deliver to you this royal letter. *(Takes it from his portfolio.)*

TELLHEIM: To me?

DISPATCH-
RIDER: According to the address . . .

MINNA: Do you hear that, Franziska? . . . The chevalier was speaking the truth after all!

DISPATCH-
RIDER: Forgive me, Major. You would have received it yesterday, but I found it impossible to track you down. It was not until today's parade that I found out your address from Lieutenant Riccaut.

FRANZISKA: Do you hear that, my Lady? . . . This is the chevalier's 'Minister. . . . How do you call the Minister out there on the big square?'

TELLHEIM: I am much obliged to you for your trouble.

DISPATCH-
RIDER: It's my duty, Major.

Exit.

SCENE SEVEN

Von Tellheim, Minna, Franziska.

TELLHEIM: Ah, my Lady, what have I here? What can this letter contain?

MINNA: It is not my place to extend my curiosity thus far.

TELLHEIM: What? You persist in separating my fate from your own? . . . But why delay in opening it? . . . It can make me no more unfortunate than I am already. No, dearest Minna, it can make us no more unfortunate than we are now; but perhaps more fortunate! Permit me, my Lady!

Opens and reads the letter, while the Landlord slips onstage.

SCENE EIGHT

Landlord, Von Tellheim, Franziska, Minna.

LANDLORD: *(To Franziska.)* Pst! a word, my pretty child!

FRANZISKA: *(Approaching him.)* Landlord? I'm sorry, we don't know
              ourselves what's in the letter.

LANDLORD: Who cares about the letter? . . . I'm coming about the
              ring. Her Ladyship must give it me back at once. Just's
              here; he wants to redeem it.

MINNA: *(Who has approached the Landlord.)* Just tell Just that it
              has already been redeemed; and tell him by whom as
              well; by me.

LANDLORD: But . . .

MINNA: I will take full responsibility. Now go.

              Exit Landlord.

SCENE NINE

Von Tellheim, Minna, Franziska.

FRANZISKA: And now, my Lady, make it up with the poor Major.

MINNA: You little peacemaker! As if the tangle must not
              unloose itself presently.

TELLHEIM: *(Having read, in great excitement.)* Ah! here too he has
              shown his true self! . . . Oh, my Lady, what justice!
              . . . What kindness! . . . This is more than I had
              anticipated! . . . More than I deserve! . . . My fortune,
              my honour, all restored to me! . . . But am I not
              dreaming? *(Looking at the letter again as if to convince
              himself.)* No, this is no longed for illusion! . . . Read it
              yourself, my Lady, read it yourself!

MINNA: I would not presume to, Major.

TELLHEIM: Presume? The letter is to me, to your Tellheim, Minna.
              It contains . . . that which your uncle cannot take from
              you. You must read it; read it!

MINNA: Well, if it will please you, Major . . . *(Takes the letter and reads.)* 'My dear Major von Tellheim. I wish you to know that the affair which led me to be solicitous as to your honour has been resolved entirely in your favour. My brother has enquired into the particulars of the case, and his evidence has proved you more than innocent. The State Treasury has orders to surrender to you the bill in question, and to repay the monies advanced. I have also commanded that all the outstanding claims of the Army Treasurers against you be cancelled. Report to me whether your health will permit you to take service again. I would be unwilling to lose a man of your valour and intelligence. I remain your well-affectioned King, etc.'

TELLHEIM: Well, what do you say to that, my Lady?

MINNA: *(Folding the letter and handing it back.)* I? Nothing.

TELLHEIM: Nothing?

MINNA: Well, yes: that your King, who is a great man, may very well also be a good man. . . . But what is that to me? He is not my king.

TELLHEIM: And you have nothing more to say? Nothing concerning ourselves?

MINNA: You will enter the service again. The major will become a lieutenant-colonel, perhaps a colonel. I heartily congratulate you.

TELLHEIM: And you know me no better than that? . . . No, now that fortune has returned to me enough to satisfy the desires of a reasonable man, it will depend on my Minna alone, whether in future I shall belong to anyone but her. May my whole life be dedicated to her service alone! The service of the great is dangerous, and does not repay the effort, the constraints and the degradation which it brings with it. Minna is not one of those vain creatures who love in their men only their titles and positions. She will love me for myself, and for her I will forget the whole world. I became a soldier for purely personal reasons; I don't know myself on what political principles; with the idea that it was good for a man of honour to try for a

period in this condition, to acquaint himself with
danger in all its forms, and to learn coolness and
determination. Only utter necessity could compel me to
make a vocation of this experiment, an occupation of
this casual employment. And now that I am under no
constraint, now I have only one ambition, and that is,
once again, to become a peaceful and contented person.
And this I have no doubt I will become with you,
dearest Minna, and in your society will remain so
perpetually. . . . Tomorrow we shall be united in the
holiest of ties; and then let us look around and find in
the whole of the inhabited earth the quietest, calmest,
pleasantest corner, that needs but a happy couple to
turn it into a paradise. There we shall live, there each
of our days. . . . What is the matter, my Lady?

*She moves uneasily hither and thither, trying to hide
her emotion.*

MINNA :   *(Composing herself.)* You are so cruel, Tellheim, to
describe so enticingly a happiness which I must deny
myself. My loss . . .

TELLHEIM :   Your loss? . . . What do you call your loss? Whatever
Minna might lose is not Minna. You are still the
sweetest, most delightful, most charming, and the best
creature under the sun; all goodness and generosity, all
innocence and joy! . . . With, now and again, a little
mischief, and here and there a little wilfulness. . . . So
much the better! So much the better! For otherwise
Minna would be an angel, whom I must worship with
trembling, but whom I could not love. *(Seizes her hand
to kiss it.)*

MINNA :   *(Drawing back her hand.)* Not so, Sir! . . . How can
you change so quickly? . . . Is this flattering, ardent
lover the restrained Tellheim? . . . Is it only the return
of his good fortune which can inflame him thus? . . .
He must allow me, in this fleeting ardour of his, to
reason for us both. . . . While he could still reason for
himself, I heard him say that it was a worthless love
which could heedlessly expose its object to
contempt. . . . Quite right, but I aspire to a love just as
pure and as noble as his. . . . And now, when his
honour calls him, and a great monarch is courting him,

should I agree to his abandoning himself to dreams of
love with me? To the glorious warrior degenerating into a
dallying shepherd? . . . No, Major, follow the signal of
your better destiny . . .

TELLHEIM: Very well! If you find the wide world more attractive,
Minna . . . very well! We shall stay in the wide world!
. . . But how small, how poverty-stricken this wide
world is! . . . As yet you only know its glittering side.
But surely, Minna, you shall. . . . So be it! Until then,
enough! There will be no lack of admirers of your
perfection, nor of those envious of my good fortune.

MINNA: No, Tellheim that was not my meaning! I was
directing you into the wide world, back on to the path
of honour, without wishing to follow you myself. . . .
There Tellheim will need an unblemished wife! A
runaway girl from Saxony, who has thrown herself at
his head . . .

TELLHEIM: *(Getting up and looking fiercely about him.)* Who would
dare to say such a thing? . . . Oh, Minna, I am afraid
of what I might do if anyone but you had said that. My
rage against them would know no bounds.

MINNA: There you are! That is precisely what troubles me. You
would not tolerate the slightest mockery of me, and yet
you would have to accept the very bitterest every
day. . . . In short, Tellheim, let me tell you what I have
firmly resolved, and from which nothing in the world
will move me . . .

TELLHEIM: Before you finish, Fräulein. . . . I implore you, Minna!
. . . Consider for another moment that you are
sentencing me to life or death!

MINNA: I need no further consideration. . . . As surely as I gave
you back the ring with which you plighted me your
troth, as surely as you took back *this* ring; so surely
shall the unfortunate Barnhelm never be the bride of
the more fortunate Tellheim!

TELLHEIM: And thus you seal my fate!

MINNA: Equality is alone the strongest bond of love. . . . The
fortunate Barnhelm wished only to live for the
fortunate Tellheim. The unfortunate Minna too would

at least have been convinced that her friend's
misfortune could be increased or alleviated by her. . . .
He perceived this before the arrival of this letter, which
once more removes any equality between us, however
much I may have seemed to hesitate still.

TELLHELM: Is it true, then, my Lady? . . . I thank you, Minna,
that you have not in fact condemned me. . . . You wish
only for the unfortunate Tellheim? He is at your
service. *(Coldly)* I now realise that it is not seemly for
me to accept this tardy justice; that it would be better
if I no longer sued for what has been robbed of all
honour for me by such shameful suspicion. . . . Yes, I
will not have received the letter. Let this be my only
reply to it! *(Goes to tear it.)*

MINNA: *(Grasps his hands.)* What do you want, Tellheim?

TELLHEIM: To possess you.

MINNA: Stop!

TELLHEIM: Fräulein, I will certainly tear it to pieces if you do not
quickly change your mind. . . . Then we shall see what
else you find to object to in me.

MINNA: What? In this tone of voice? . . . Shall I then, must I
then appear despicable in my own eyes? Never! It is a
worthless creature who is not ashamed to owe all her
happiness to the blind tenderness of a man.

TELLHEIM: That's false, utterly false!

MINNA: Will you venture to condemn your own words in my
mouth?

TELLHEIM: Sophistress! Is then the weaker sex dishonoured by
everything which would not become the stronger?
Should a man then allow himself everything which
befits a woman? Which did Nature appoint to be the
support of the other?

MINNA: Calm yourself, Tellheim! . . . I will not be wholly
without protection, even if I must decline the honour
of yours. So much must remain to me as necessity
demands. I have sent my card to our consul here. He
will see me today. I am hoping he will look after my
interests. But time is passing. Permit me, Major . . .

TELLHEIM: I shall accompany you, my Lady.

MINNA: Not now, Major. Leave me . . .

TELLHEIM: Your shadow will leave you sooner than I will!
Wherever you may go, and whomever you may meet,
everywhere I will tell the tale, a hundred times a day,
I will tell them what bonds tie you to me, and by what
cruel obstinacy you seek to sever these bonds . . .

SCENE TEN

Just, Von Tellheim, Minna, Franziska.

JUST: *(Impetuously)* Major! Major!

TELLHEIM: Well?

JUST: Come quickly, quickly!

TELLHEIM: What? Come here! Tell me what is the matter?

JUST: Listen . . . *(Whispers to him.)*

MINNA: *(Meanwhile to Franziska.)* Did you notice anything,
Franziska?

FRANZISKA: You're merciless! I've been standing here on pins and
needles!

TELLHEIM: *(To Just.)* What are you saying? . . . That is not
possible! . . . Her? *(Looking wildly at Minna.)* Say it
aloud; tell her to her face! . . . . Now listen to this, my
Lady . . .

JUST: The Landlord says that Fräulein von Barnhelm herself
redeemed the ring which I pledged with him. She
recognised it as yours, and would not give it back.

TELLHEIM: Is this true, my Lady? . . . No, this cannot be true!

MINNA: *(Smiling)* And why not, Tellheim? Why can this not be
true?

TELLHEIM: *(Heatedly)* Well then, let it be true! . . . What an awful
light suddenly dawns on me. . . . Now I see her for
what she is . . . false and faithless!

MINNA: *(Shocked)* Who? Who is faithless?

TELLHEIM: She whom I will no longer name.

MINNA: Tellheim!

TELLHEIM: Forget my name! . . . You came here in order to break with me. That is clear. How willing chance is to come to the aid of the faithless! It brought your own ring into your hands, and your cunning contrived to put my ring in mine.

MINNA: Tellheim, what ghosts are you seeing? Compose yourself and listen to me.

FRANZISKA: *(To herself.)* Now let her have it!

SCENE ELEVEN

Werner (with a bag of gold), Von Tellheim, Minna, Franziska, Just.

WERNER: Here I am, Major.

TELLHEIM: *(Not looking at him.)* Who sent for you?

WERNER: Here's the money: a thousand Pistoles!

TELLHEIM: I don't want it!

WERNER: Tomorrow, Major, you can command as much again, and more.

TELLHEIM: Keep your money!

WERNER: But it's really your money, Major. I don't think you've seen who you're talking to.

TELLHEIM: Take it away, I said.

WERNER: What's wrong? . . . It's Werner.

TELLHEIM: All kindness is pretence, all service treachery.

WERNER: Does that include me?

TELLHEIM: As you like.

WERNER: I have only been carrying out your orders . . .

TELLHEIM: Then carry out this one: Clear off!

WERNER: *(Angrily)* Major, I'm a man . . .

TELLHEIM: Well, that's all right then.

WERNER: Who has a temper . . .

TELLHEIM: Good! Temper is the best thing we have.

WERNER: Please, Major . . .

TELLHEIM: How many more times must I say it? I have no use for your money!

WERNER: Well, let him use it who will! *(Throws the bag at his feet and steps aside.)*

MINNA: *(To Franziska.)* My dear Franziska, I should have taken your advice. I have carried the joke too far. . . . But let him hear me at least . . . *(Goes to him.)*

FRANZISKA: *(Does not answer, but approaches Werner.)* Sergeant-Major! . . .

WERNER: *(Sullenly)* Go away!

FRANZISKA: Huh! What kind of gentlemen are these?

MINNA: Tellheim! . . . Tellheim! . . . *(He bites his fingers in anger, his face turned away, not listening.)* No! That is too severe. Listen to me! . . . You are deceiving yourself! . . . A simple misunderstanding. . . . Tellheim. . . . will you not listen to your Minna? . . . Can you entertain such a suspicion? . . . That I should want to break with you? . . . That I should have come here for that? . . . Tellheim!

SCENE TWELVE

Two Servants (running from opposite sides), Werner, Von Tellheim, Just, Minna, Franziska.

FIRST
SERVANT: Your Ladyship, His Excellency the Count!

SECOND
SERVANT: He has arrived, your Ladyship!

FRANZISKA: *(Running to the window.)* It's him!

MINNA: Is it him? . . . Now, quickly, Tellheim . . .

TELLHEIM: *(Suddenly comes to himself again.)* Who? Who is
              coming? Your uncle, Fräulein? Your terrible uncle?
              Just let him come, just let him come! . . . Have no fear!
              He will not offend you with so much as a glance! He
              will have me to deal with. . . . But you do not deserve
              it of me . . .

MINNA: Quickly, embrace me, Tellheim, and forget
              everything . . .

TELLHEIM: Ha! If only I thought you could regret it.

MINNA: No, I cannot regret having gained this glimpse into the
              centre of your heart. Ah, what a man you are! . . .
              Embrace your Minna, your fortunate Minna, but in
              nothing more fortunate than in having you. . . . *(Falls
              into his arms.)* And now to meet him!

TELLHEIM: Who?

MINNA: The best of your unknown friends.

TELLHEIM: What?

MINNA: The Count, my uncle, my father, your father. . . . My
              flight, his ill-will, my disinheritance . . . did you not
              realise it was all an invention? You credulous knight!

TELLHEIM: An invention? But the ring? The ring!

MINNA: Where have you put the ring I gave back to you?

TELLHEIM: So you will receive it again. . . . I am so happy. . . .
              Here, Minna . . . *(Takes it out.)*

MINNA: But look at it first! . . . None so blind as those who will
              not see! Which ring is it, then? The one I had from
              you, or the one you had from me? Is it not the very
              one I would not leave in the hands of the landlord?

TELLHEIM: My God! What am I seeing? What am I hearing?

MINNA: Shall I take it once more? Shall I? . . . Give it me,
              give it me! *(Snatches it and puts it on his finger herself.)*
              Well now, is everything ready?

TELLHEIM: Where am I? . . . *(Kissing her hand.)* Oh, you
              mischievous angel . . . to torment me so!

MINNA: Let that be a warning to you, dear husband, never to

play a trick on me, without expecting me to play one
on you directly. . . Do you think that did not torment
me too?

TELLHEIM: You little actresses! I ought to have known you better.

FRANZISKA: No, really; I'm no good as an actress. I was shaking
and quivering, and I had to use my hand to keep my
mouth closed at times.

MINNA: Mine was not an easy role to play either. But come
now!

TELLHEIM: I am not fully recovered yet. . . . I feel well, but so
fearful! Just like a man waking suddenly from a
terrifying dream!

MINNA: We must not delay. . . . I can hear him already.

SCENE THIRTEEN

*Count von Bruchsall with several servants, Landlord, Werner, Von
Tellheim, Just, Minna, Franziska.*

COUNT: *(Entering)* She is arrived safely, then?

MINNA: *(Rushing to him.)* Oh, Father!

COUNT: Here I am, dear Minna! *(Embracing her.)* But what's
this, my girl? *(Aware of Tellheim.)* Not here twenty-
four hours, and already you have acquaintances,
company?

MINNA: Can you guess who it is?

COUNT: It's not your Tellheim?

MINNA: Who else should it be? . . . Come, Tellheim! *(Leading
him to the Count.)*

COUNT: Well, Sir; we have never met before, but at first sight I
thought I recognised you. I hoped it might be so. . . .
Embrace me. . . . You have my deepest respect. I ask
for your friendship. . . . My niece, my daughter loves
you . . .

MINNA: That you know, Father . . . and is it blind, this love of
mine?

COUNT:	No, Minna, your love is not blind, but your lover is dumb.
TELLHEIM:	*(Throwing himself into the Count's arms.)* Let me come to my senses again, my . . . Father!
COUNT:	Yes, my Son! I can see that if your mouth is dumb, yet your heart speaks still. . . . As a rule, I am not fond of officers in these colours, *(Pointing to Tellheim's uniform)* but you are an honourable man, Tellheim, and whatever clothes an honourable man may wear, we must still love him.
MINNA:	Oh, if only you knew the whole story! . . .
COUNT:	What is there to prevent me hearing it? . . . Where are my rooms, Landlord?
LANDLORD:	Might I ask your Excellency to do me the honour of stepping this way?
COUNT:	Come, Minna! Come, Major!
	Exit with Landlord and servants.
MINNA:	Come, Tellheim!
TELLHEIM:	I will follow you in a moment, my Lady. I just want a few words with this fellow. *(Turning to Werner.)*
MINNA:	Yes, good. It's high time, is it not, Franziska?
	Exit after Count.

SCENE FOURTEEN

Von Tellheim, Werner, Just, Franziska.

TELLHEIM:	*(Pointing to the money bag thrown down by Werner.)* Here, Just . . . pick up that bag and take it home; go on!
	Exit Just with bag.
WERNER:	*(Still sullenly in a corner, appearing to take no part, hears this.)* Well then!
TELLHEIM:	*(Familiarly, going to him.)* Werner, when can I have the other thousand Pistoles?

WERNER: *(Suddenly in a good mood again.)* Tomorrow, Major,
             tomorrow.

TELLHEIM: I have no need to be your debtor, but I will act as your
             treasurer. Good-hearted people like you should all be
             given guardians. In your way you are a kind of
             spendthrift, you know. . . . We fell out over that only
             recently, Werner!

WERNER: On my soul, you're right. . . . But I really shouldn't
             have been such a blockhead. I can see that now. I
             deserve a hundred lashes. You'd be welcome to give
             them to me yourself, if it meant that there'd be no
             more bad feeling between us, my dear Major!

TELLHEIM: Bad feeling? . . . *(Clasps his hand.)* Read in my eyes all
             that I cannot put into words for you! . . . Ha! I'd like
             to meet the man who has a better sweetheart, and a
             truer than I! . . . Don't you agree, Franziska? . . .

                  Exit.

SCENE FIFTEEN

Werner, Franziska.

FRANZISKA: *(To herself.)* He's right, he really *is* too good a man! . . .
             I won't find another like him. . . . I must say it! *(Shyly
             and abashed approaches Werner.)* Sergeant-Major? . . .

WERNER: *(Wiping his eyes.)* Well? . . .

FRANZISKA: Sergeant-Major . . .

WERNER: What do you want, then, Little Lady?

FRANZISKA: Look at me a minute, Sergeant-Major . . .

WERNER: I can't just now. I don't know what's got into my eyes.

FRANZISKA: Look at me, I said!

WERNER: I'm afraid I've done too much of that already, Little
             Lady! . . . Well then, I'm looking at you now. What is
             it?

FRANZISKA: Mr Sergeant-Major . . . don't you need a Mrs
             Sergeant-Major?

WERNER: Are you serious, Little Lady?

FRANZISKA: Of course!

WERNER: Would you take off with me to Persia?

FRANZISKA: Anywhere you like.

WERNER: Really? . . . Hey there, Major! You can boast! Now
             I've a sweetheart who's just as good as yours, and a
             friend who's just as true! . . . Give me your hand,
             Little Lady! Done! . . . In ten years you'll be a
             general's wife . . . or a widow!

THE END